ASSESSING STUDENT LEARNING OUTCOMES IN THE COLLEGE ENVIRONMENT

Angela Albert

ASSESSING STUDENT LEARNING OUTCOMES IN THE COLLEGE ENVIRONMENT

Effective Methods of Measuring General Education Programs' Core Learning Outcomes at Urban and Metropolitan Universities

VDM Verlag Dr. Müller

Impressum/Imprint (nur für Deutschland/ only for Germany)

Bibliografische Information der Deutschen Nationalbibliothek: Die Deutsche Nationalbibliothek verzeichnet diese Publikation in der Deutschen Nationalbibliografie; detaillierte bibliografische Daten sind im Internet über http://dnb.d-nb.de abrufbar.

Alle in diesem Buch genannten Marken und Produktnamen unterliegen warenzeichen-, marken- oder patentrechtlichem Schutz bzw. sind Warenzeichen oder eingetragene Warenzeichen der jeweiligen Inhaber. Die Wiedergabe von Marken, Produktnamen, Gebrauchsnamen, Handelsnamen, Warenbezeichnungen u.s.w. in diesem Werk berechtigt auch ohne besondere Kennzeichnung nicht zu der Annahme, dass solche Namen im Sinne der Warenzeichen- und Markenschutzgesetzgebung als frei zu betrachten wären und daher von jedermann benutzt werden dürften.

Coverbild: www.purestockx.com

Verlag: VDM Verlag Dr. Müller Aktiengesellschaft & Co. KG
Dudweiler Landstr. 99, 66123 Saarbrücken, Deutschland
Telefon +49 681 9100-698, Telefax +49 681 9100-988, Email: info@vdm-verlag.de
Zugl.: Orlando, Diss., 2004

Herstellung in Deutschland:
Schaltungsdienst Lange o.H.G., Berlin
Books on Demand GmbH, Norderstedt
Reha GmbH, Saarbrücken
Amazon Distribution GmbH, Leipzig
ISBN: 978-3-639-08458-0

Imprint (only for USA, GB)

Bibliographic information published by the Deutsche Nationalbibliothek: The Deutsche Nationalbibliothek lists this publication in the Deutsche Nationalbibliografie; detailed bibliographic data are available in the Internet at http://dnb.d-nb.de .

Any brand names and product names mentioned in this book are subject to trademark, brand or patent protection and are trademarks or registered trademarks of their respective holders. The use of brand names, product names, common names, trade names, product descriptions etc. even without a particular marking in this works is in no way to be construed to mean that such names may be regarded as unrestricted in respect of trademark and brand protection legislation and could thus be used by anyone.

Cover image: www.purestockx.com

Publisher:
VDM Verlag Dr. Müller Aktiengesellschaft & Co. KG
Dudweiler Landstr. 99, 66123 Saarbrücken, Germany
Phone +49 681 9100-698, Fax +49 681 9100-988, Email: info@vdm-publishing.com

Printed in the U.S.A.
Printed in the U.K. by (see last page)
ISBN: 978-3-639-08458-0

ACKNOWLEDGMENTS

When I decided to embark on my doctoral studies in the Spring 2001 semester, I made the decision realizing that not only was I beginning a new adventure but that my husband and children would be integrally involved in the process as well. Before I extend my gratitude to them, I would like to acknowledge a few other people who participated in this adventure.

First, I extend my appreciation to Dr. Mary Ann Lynn who started me out in the research process. Second, Dr. Levester Tubbs, thank you for your ongoing guidance. Thank you for the final push, which ensured my successful completion of this arduous task. Finally, I owe a debt of gratitude to my committee members for their mentoring, support, and encouragement. I extend my gratitude to Drs. Laura Blasi, Michael Johnson, George Pawlas, Kenyatta Rivers, and Janice Terrell.

I would be remiss if I did not extend my appreciation to my co-workers (Ev, Laura, Pat, Kathy, Hector, Basma, Uday, Ysela) and supervisor (Julia) for lending a hand in many small ways. Those small things really added up and I will never forget you for the kind deeds.

To my sister Delia, my brothers Lindsey, Brooks, and Avery, thank you for your prayers, love, and for having faith in me to continue being excellent in all that I do.

I am forever thankful to the woman (Mrs. Delia McKnight) who gave me life and to the father (Mr. Horace McKnight) who has brought joy into my mother's life, as well as protection and a sense of stability to my entire family. Thank you both for trusting that I could get this job done. Never once did you question if I could do it. Mom, I owe all that I am to you. Thanks for teaching me to have an abiding love for God, an eternal love for my family, and an appreciation for the importance of hard work. It does pay off. Mom, you are my rock; you are the dearest Mom anyone could ever have.

i

Thanks to my beautiful children, Jabreale, Joseph, and Dee Dee. Thanks for hanging in there with me and never, ever using me for an excuse to not do your very best in school and in other extracurricular activities. You are the world's greatest children.

Larry, you mean more to me than anyone could ever know. You were steadfast in your patience, love, and affection. You just plain old kept putting up with my temperamental self. I love you for surprising me and never complaining or giving up. You were there all the way, taking care of what needed to be done. You even endured my defense.

Finally, I dedicate this work to my eldest brother and sister. These two loves of my life passed away within the last 18 months of this study. It was difficult to stay focused, but with God's help and in honor of my family's tradition of excellence, I did. May you rest in peace, Walter Lee and Vivian Yvonne. I miss you beyond anyone's imagination but feel confident that you are looking down from heaven and smiling.

TABLE OF CONTENTS

LIST OF TABLES

CHAPTER 1

INTRODUCTION

In 2001–2002, there were 4,197 accredited, degree-granting institutions in the United States (National Center for Education Statistics [NCES], 2002). The data for 2000 indicate that there were 15.3 million students enrolled in degree-granting institutions (Frank Morgan, personal communication, August 14, 2003). These colleges and universities have become increasingly committed to educating themselves on how best to assess student learning in their undergraduate programs, specifically general education (Gaff, 1999; Palomba, 2002).

Purpose

This study was conducted primarily to add to the current knowledge in the area of general education assessment. It is worth noting that the identification of methods of measurement leading to accurate data that can be used for improvement in general education remains difficult (Brown & Glasner, 1999; Pike, 2002).

Ewell (1995) found that authentic, creative, and action-oriented assessment approaches are ignited by two key factors:

> a) taken from the proper value perspective, assessment constitutes a powerful tool for collective improvement that is highly consistent with core academic values and b) infusion of the logic of assessment directly into classroom and curricular settings is perhaps the most powerful means we have at our disposal to transform the logic of pedagogy itself—from one-way instruction to collaboration and partnership. (p.147)

Assessment, if conducted effectively, leads to the discovery of weaknesses within the curriculum, instructional methods, and faculty preparedness (Palomba & Banta, 1999). Assessment may also lead to verification of what is working in educational practices. Faculty

1

members who have been accustomed to a culture of academic freedom may find it difficult to share assessment findings with all constituencies for fear of repercussions. Because of this common sentiment, faculty members must be assured that the purpose of assessment is for continuous improvement (Huba & Freed, 2000). This study will contribute to furthering understanding about methods that provide higher education with useful information about its educational practices.

Problem Statement

The purpose of this study was to determine (a) what instruments and methods of data collection are being used to assess core general education student-learning outcomes at urban and metropolitan universities and (b) the extent to which these approaches to measurement are producing data that can be used for improvement purposes.

Definition of Terms

The following terms were used in this study:

General Education: "The approximately one-third of the collegiate four years that complements the one-third devoted to the major course of study and the other one-third that is related to the major area" (Miller, 1990, p. 119). General education is the part of the curriculum that provides students with knowledge that can enhance their success in maneuvering in society.

Assessment: The systematic collection, review, and use of information about educational programs for the purpose of improving student learning and development. This process serves instruction and learning by communicating the strengths (areas of the curriculum that students are achieving at expectations) and weaknesses (areas of the curriculum that students are below

2

target level of expectation) of students. It also provides information about the curriculum and suggests areas that need improvement (Kiger, 1996; Palomba & Banta, 1999).

Assessment Strategy: A method that is used to measure students' performance on a specific measurable learning outcome. Maki (2001) explained that identifying appropriate assessment strategies requires a comprehensive understanding of what each method measures and how it connects to intended outcomes and agreed-upon levels of student performance.

Traditional Assessment Strategies: The historical and conventional methods of measuring learning outcomes, typically standardized tests (Banta, Lund, Black & Oblander, 1996). Examples of these strategies are the Collegiate Assessment of Academic Proficiency (CAAP) and the Academic Profile offered by the Educational Testing Service (ETS).

Alternative Assessment Strategies: The unconventional methods of measuring student-learning outcomes. Strategies may include, but are not limited to, locally developed tests, course-based assessment, multi-course or theme-based assessment, self-assessment, portfolios, focus groups, and capstone courses (Maki, 2001).

Core Student-Learning Outcome: A student's cognitive gain, general maturation, and attitudinal development. These high-level outcomes are the primary concerns of the general education curriculum. They typically relate to areas such as critical thinking, problem solving, quantitative skills, global perspectives, verbal skills, diversity, wellness, library skills, and others.

AAHE: The American Association of Higher Education, an "organization that serves its members, other individuals, communities, and institutions in the higher-education community by building their capacity as learners and leaders and increasing their effectiveness in a complex, interconnected world" (American Association of Higher Education [AAHE], 2004). The

3

association equips individuals and institutions committed to such changes with the knowledge they need to foster those changes.

The Coalition of Urban and Metropolitan Colleges and Universities (CUMU): "The Coalition of Urban and Metropolitan Universities brings together universities that share the mission of striving for national excellence while contributing to the economic development, social health, and cultural vitality of the urban or metropolitan centers served" (Coalition of Urban and Metropolitan Colleges and Universities [CUMU], n.d.). Currently, 62 voluntary member institutions make up the coalition. Characteristics of these institutions are that they strive to be responsive to the needs of their communities, to include teaching that is aligned with the varying needs of students, and to build mutually rewarding relationships with elementary and secondary schools. These institutions of higher learning combine research-based learning with practical application. They are devoted to establishing interdisciplinary partnerships and forming alliances with external public and private organizations in an effort to assist in solving complex metropolitan problems. Within the university environment, these institutions strive to motivate and educate students to become informed and engaged citizens who play a role in the well-being of society.

Delimitations

The delimitations of this study were as follows:

1. The study was delimited to the responses of faculty members and administrators who serve in a leadership capacity in the area of general education assessment at institutions that are members of The Coalition of Urban and Metropolitan Universities.

4

2. Responses used in data analysis were limited to those that were obtained in response to questionnaires and structured telephone interviews. Data on general education goals of institutions, student-learning outcomes, measurement approaches, and changes were gathered using a questionnaire designed by the researcher. Additionally, data were gathered via structured phone interviews based on the original instrument's content, literature provided by the respondent on the institution's general education initiative, and websites of the colleges and universities.

Assumptions

The following statements stipulate the assumptions of this study:

1. It was assumed that the survey instrument was appropriate to obtain respondents' answers to questions regarding the general education assessment process being implemented in their institutions.

2. It was assumed that the faculty and administrators provided honest answers to the survey instrument.

3. It was assumed that the respondents and the researcher had the same basic understanding of the terminology used in the instrument.

4. It was assumed that responses provided accurate and reliable data about the assessment strategies that are known to be in use for general education within the targeted institutions of higher education.

Significance of the Study

The Association of American Colleges and Universities (AAC&U) (2001) noted that there are more than 850 institutional members in the organization, including those classified by the Carnegie Commission on Higher Education as liberal-arts colleges, two-year colleges, research and doctoral-granting universities, master's-degree-granting colleges and universities, professional universities, and systems offices. These institutions (independent and public, large and small, rural and urban, and residential and commuter) serve students across the United States. Membership in AAC&U is an expression of the institution's belief in the significance of a liberal education for all students (Association of American Colleges & Universities [AAC&U] Website, n.d.; Esther Merves, Director for Membership, AAC&U, personal communication, June 23, 2003). Gaff (1999) noted that the AAC&U has assisted approximately 1,000 institutions in revitalizing their general education programs and acknowledged that "signs of progress can be seen in a variety of areas, including campus task forces on general education assessment projects on the core curriculum, and a range of related curricular and faculty development initiatives" (p. i).

The significance of this study is that it contributes to the body of knowledge on assessment in the area of general education. Ratcliff, Johnson, La Nasa, and Gaff (2000) presented data from their survey administered to AAC&U members. The data indicated that only 15% of the institutions that responded to the survey who are initiating change in the curriculum of general education programs are assessing student outcomes. Essentially, these institutions are depriving themselves of valuable data and information that might make their organizational changes more meaningful.

6

1. The results of this study will assist assessment practitioners in identifying core student-learning outcomes that are appropriate for measurement in metropolitan and urban institutions.

2. The results of this study will assist assessment practitioners in identifying measurement approaches that, if implemented, may be effective in contributing to an understanding about the efficacy of educational practices in general education.

3. The results of this study will generally add to the current knowledge base on assessment in higher education, specifically assessment of general education student-learning outcomes within the metropolitan and urban institutional context.

Conceptual Framework

A Brief Overview of the History of General Education

General education dates back to colonial America when education of clergymen and lawyers was the primary purpose for institutions of higher learning (Miller, 1990). From the early 1900s to the 1970s, little innovation in general education requirements occurred.

Harvard University, a leader in higher education issues during this period, published the classic 1945 Harvard red book (developed by the Harvard Committee). A prescription for an exemplary general education program was offered, which included four goals for students: (a) students should think effectively, (b) students should be able to communicate thought, (c) students should be able to make relevant judgments, and (d) students should be able to distinguish among values (Miller, 1990).

In 1979, a document compiled by the same committee from Harvard University added to the 1945 report by including two new dimensions: depth in some field of knowledge and intercultural awareness. In this report, greater emphasis was placed on written communication. The report also stated that students should be exposed to six core areas: foreign culture, moral reasoning, social analysis, historical study, literature and arts, and science (Miller, 1990).

Palomba and Banta (1999) noted that, historically, general education focused on exposure to many skills and attitudes that enhanced students' ability to be successful in society. Undergraduate education is a context within which young adults develop social skills necessary for success in a contemporary society filled with complex bureaucracies.

Mayhew, Ford, and Hubbard (1990) found that there was a major decline of general education programs beginning in the 1960s. They and Gaff (1999) explained that this time period led the Carnegie Foundation for the Advancement of Teaching to proclaim the collegiate experience a "disaster area." There was a distinct change in the perception of higher education's role and responsibility in meeting the needs of diverse groups (e.g., minority students who had never had access to college, the economically disadvantaged, women). Some consequences that surfaced with the admission of diverse groups were modification in educational requirements, implementation of remedial services, and approval of academic credit for courses with only high school–level content.

Miller (1990) asserted that around 1977, a need to revisit general education requirements was sparked by several factors, including "increasing enrollments in professional programs, increasing professionalization of liberal arts colleges, rising costs of education, and growing interest in adult education" (p. 118).

Miller (1990) believed that after the well-known Watergate incident, some educators viewed general education as a way (a) to institute moral training for students, (b) to counter neo-isolationism ideals, (c) to counter the new narcissism, (d) to address declining performance, (e) to address a high interest in vocational careers, and (f) to address campus personnel problems. These factors all contributed to the reform of general education.

In the late 1970s, a number of colleges and universities worked toward a revival of intellectual cohesiveness in the undergraduate curriculum and the enhancement of the academic challenge. Harvard University's arts and sciences faculty approved new graduation requirements to ensure students' exposure to the major domains of knowledge (Miller, 1990). Stanford University reassessed the need to include courses in western culture and made the subject a requirement for all students (Miller). Mayhew et al. (1990) stated that the societal changes that stemmed from economic, cultural, and global catalysts forced faculty to rethink what students should know and think upon college graduation.

Bauer and Frawley (2002) reported that in the 21st century there was a renewed emphasis on general education in colleges and universities. They stressed that although it was important for students to gain sufficient knowledge and skills in their chosen field of study (e.g., nursing, performing arts, engineering), it was imperative that students gain a broader education in the areas of writing skills, mathematics, critical thinking, problem solving, and values and attitudes, among others.

The Emergence of Assessment of General Education

Huba and Freed (2000) defined assessment as:

the process of gathering and discussing information from multiple and diverse sources in order to develop a deep understanding of what students know, understand, and can do with their knowledge as a result of their educational experiences; the process culminates when assessment results are used to improve subsequent learning. (p. viii)

According to Huba and Freed (2000), there were two primary reasons for the increased attention to assessment in higher education: the need for increased accountability and the need

9

for continuous improvement. Public and political leaders engaged in discussions regarding the quality of education. The general agreement was that education was declining rapidly. This decline provided the impetus during the 1960s to reform higher education at all levels.

By the 1970s, higher education was in a financial crisis (Miller, 1990). Available resources were scarce and were not keeping pace with escalating costs and inflation. In addition, student demographics were changing dramatically, and adjustments were being made to accommodate those differences. Miller noted that out of this movement, accountability concerns continued to evolve. The concomitant need to improve learning through modifying the curriculum design and other aspects of higher education was also recognized and addressed.

Society's expectation had been not only that institutions of higher learning would prepare students to work within an academic setting, but also that they would sufficiently equip students with the knowledge and skills that would enable them to perform effectively in business, in technology, in service industries, and in society at large (Ewell, 1995). Ewell also stated that one of the most effective means for publicizing how well higher education is progressing has been to publish data that reflect what is actually being accomplished.

This strategy has been useful in improving the image of higher education. It is also emerging as an expectation of state legislation that strengthens accountability through a linkage with funding (Banta et al., 1996; Callahan, Doyle, & Finney, 2001; Ewell, 2001). Palomba and Banta (1999) asserted that "the dual nature of assessment, to both improve programs and communicate with the public, should be utilized" (p. xviii).

A review of the literature revealed that scholars of assessment have been consistent in their belief that it is important for colleges and universities to improve their processes when students are not achieving up to the standards that have been set (Banta et al., 1996; Ewell, 1995,

2002; Huba & Freed, 2000; Kuh, 2001; Maki, 2002). These same students can become

significant contributors in the workplace, but only if they acquire important skills and knowledge

that are essential in their chosen careers. The number of students who are leaving college without

necessary skills, knowledge, and expertise is a major problem for all who have a stake in the

well-being and progress of society (Banta et al., 1996; Cornesky, 1993; Hubbard, 1993).

Posovac and Carey (1997) elaborated on the fact that developing learning outcomes and

measuring and reviewing academic programs' learning outcomes have become an integral part of

the institution's effectiveness initiative mandated by accrediting bodies. The Southern

Association of Colleges and Schools (SACS), one of seven accrediting bodies of institutions of

higher learning, has outlined core requirements for accreditation, focusing on assessment of

academic programs. Core Requirement 5 requires an institution to

> engage in ongoing, integrated, and institution-wide research-based planning and
> evaluation processes that incorporate a systematic review of programs and services that
> (a) results in continuing improvement and (b) demonstrates that the institution is
> effectively accomplishing its mission. (Commission on Colleges—Southern
> Accreditation of Colleges and Schools [SACS] Website, n.d.)

Under SACS' Comprehensive Standards (Commission on Colleges, 2004), Educational

Programs Standard #3.5.2 states that "the institution awards degrees only to those students who

have earned at least 25 percent of the credit hours required for the degree through instruction

offered by that institution" (p. 7).

The North Central Association of Colleges and Schools is an accrediting body that

accredits colleges and schools in 19 states—Arizona, Arkansas, Colorado, Illinois, Indiana,

Iowa, Kansas, Michigan, Minnesota, Missouri, Nebraska, New Mexico, North Dakota, Ohio,

Oklahoma, South Dakota, West Virginia, Wisconsin, and Wyoming—and Department of

Defense schools and Navajo Nation schools. This agency stipulates in Criterion #3 that the institution is required to demonstrate that it is accomplishing its educational and other purposes. Colleges and universities are also required to conduct assessment and to document the following:

1. Assessment of appropriate student academic achievement

2. Proficiency in skills and competencies essential for all college-educated adults

3. Completion of an identifiable and coherent undergraduate-level general education component

4. Mastery of the level of knowledge appropriate to the degree granted

5. Control by the institution's faculty of evaluation of student-learning and granting of academic credit (p. 9)

Meeting accreditation criteria is only one purpose for the focus of higher education on assessment. Institutions have also realized the value of assessment for other equally important reasons, such as program accreditation, performance-based funding, strategic planning, and continuous improvement. The demands for a higher level of sophistication and appropriateness in assessment methods have dramatically increased (Ewell, 2001; Maki, 2001; Pike, 2002).

In 1990, President George Bush and state governors emphasized the need to focus on the country's educational goals for students enrolled in institutions of higher learning (NCES, 2000). These goals included the abilities to think critically, solve problems, and communicate. In response to this announcement, 500 faculty members, representing various states across the country, collaborated to compile a list of skills needed in order to demonstrate that students possessed these abilities.

On a national scale, faculty members who had roles in planning, implementing, and assessing general education included these goals and encouraged other institutions to consider including these goals into their curricula. This group also worked toward identifying experiences

12

that would lead to students' acquisition of knowledge and skills that directly related to these goals (NCES, 2000).

Palomba and Banta (1999) stated that "assessment plays a vital role in helping to determine whether general education programs are achieving their purposes and, of equal importance, helping these programs evolve and improve" (p. 241).

According to Bauer and Frawley (2002), a clear, concise assessment plan within undergraduate studies must be based on an understanding of the institution's goals for general education and how those goals fit into the mission of the institution. Additionally, faculty and other planners must be aware of how general education is merged into the curriculum and co-curriculum. It is critical for the success of the revitalization of general education that faculty and other stakeholders understand how appropriate assessment methods can be effective in light of the vast differences among institutions' students and programs (Palomba & Banta, 1999).

As a result of employers' heightened expectations for general education, college departments and programs have been compelled to reinforce specific qualities in the curricula (Miller, 1990). An example of this is an engineering program that, though primarily concerned with the technical aspects of the program, may also address a broad communication learning outcome with the following goal: Students will be able to describe to a lay audience the concepts of industrial engineering as those concepts relate to constructing a waterway (Palomba & Banta, 1999).

Identification of Appropriate Assessment Strategies

Palomba and Banta (1999) concluded that the most important selection criterion for identifying effective assessment measures is determining if the method of measurement will yield useful information that will identify weaknesses in the program. Assessment can also verify

13

strengths within the teaching and learning environment. If weaknesses are revealed through conducting assessment, then focused changes can be made in those weak areas. Ewell (2001) contended that assessment practitioners should also appreciate the importance of choosing strategies for measuring students' performance that are appropriate for the state's culture and history. He expressed the belief that "what works well in Tennessee and Florida, for a wide variety of organizational and cultural reasons, may not work elsewhere" (p. xxii).

Matching assessment strategies with specific intended learning outcomes requires an understanding of what each strategy measures and how the results relate to the agreed-upon goals of the institution and of general education. They must also relate to agreed-upon levels of student performance (Maki, 2001).

Scholars of assessment have expressed the belief that standardized tests intended to measure general education learning outcomes and the quality of education on a large-scale basis have been inadequate (Ewell, 2001; Kuh, 2001; Maki, 2001). In light of this fast-growing concern, it is disturbing to many assessment practitioners that few-to-no new test instruments have been added to the existing inventory of instruments within the past ten years (Maki, 2001).

In the comprehensive general education arena, the following four instruments have typically been used: (a) the Collegiate Assessment of Academic Proficiency (CAAP), (b) the Academic Profile offered by the Educational Testing Service (ETS), (c) ACT's no-longer-supported College Outcomes Measures Project (COMP), and (d) the University of Missouri's College-Base Examination (Ewell, 2001). There has been increasing pressure to identify and appropriately assess skills that are not as academic in nature, such as problem-solving, communication, and technical skills sought after by the employment community (Banta et al., 1996).

To bridge the existing gap between the identification of learning outcomes and appropriate assessment instruments, it is essential that multiple tools be used to gain a comprehensive understanding of students' learning. This process requires the use of standardized tests and alternative methods of assessment (Maki, 2001).

The present study addressed ways in which faculty members and administrators responded to the need to improve assessment strategies related to general education. It also concentrated on the importance of establishing sound learning outcomes with meaningful rationales, the identification of appropriate assessment methods, and the use of assessment results to make changes. The study concluded by highlighting differences that existed among the institutions involved in this study relative to learning outcomes and measurement approaches (e.g., instruments, data collection methods).

Research Questions

1. What core general education student-learning outcomes are being assessed at urban and metropolitan colleges and universities?

2. What instruments and methods of data collection are being used to assess core general education student-learning outcomes at urban and metropolitan colleges and universities?

3. Which, if any, of the current measurement approaches being used have made it possible to improve general education (curricula, specific courses, and teaching strategies)?

4. What differences, if any, exist in the institutions' stated intended core student-learning outcomes based on the type (four-year and graduate level) and size of the institution?

5. What differences, if any, exist in the usefulness of instruments and methods of data collection based on the type (four-year and graduate level) and size of the institution?

Organization of the Study

Chapter 1 introduced the problem statement and its design components. Chapter 2 reviews the literature and related research relevant to the problem of this study. Chapter 3 describes the methodology and procedures that were used for data collection and analysis. Chapter 4 describes and presents the analysis of the data gathered. Chapter 5 provides a summary and discussion of the findings, conclusions of this study, implications for assessment practices, and recommendations for future research.

CHAPTER 2

REVIEW OF THE LITERATURE

Introduction

The purpose of this chapter is to discuss the significance of general education program assessment at institutions of higher learning. The first section of this chapter provides a brief historical perspective of the general education program. The chapter further describes prevailing characteristics of general education programs across the United States. The researcher continues in the following section by discussing the importance of quality in higher education and faculty's role in the effectiveness of assessment of general education. A discussion of assessment that leads to improvement and a detailed outline of the basic principles of strong general education programs follow. The chapter then focuses on the scholarship of assessment and the critical issues involved in identifying core student-learning outcomes. Further exploration of the learning process and methodologies that measure student learning are also discussed. The chapter continues by discussing the importance of using assessment methods that yield meaningful data and ultimately in making needed changes. The researcher closes this chapter by discussing some of the changes that can be expected within higher education if assessment is conducted effectively.

History of General Education

Dressel and Mayhew (1954) and Abrahamson and Kimsey (2002) reported that the general education movement originated as a reaction against overspecialization. The movement was also propelled by the need to avoid compartmentalization that was a result of a narrow focus without ample consideration of the purpose of the curriculum. The establishment of objectives for general education programs has served as the impetus for curriculum development and has created commonality among general education curricula across the United States.

Dressel and Mayhew (1950) stated that there are three distinct general education program objectives:

1. Content orientation, wherein the primary concern is with the importance of the materials selected, and the task of education is to expose students to these materials.

2. Intellectual orientation, wherein attention focuses on certain intellectual objectives, and subject matter is selected in part because of its relevance to the attainment of these objectives.

3. Student orientation, wherein the primary value is the total development of each individual and wherein experiences are developed or selected with this end in mind. (p. 17)

They also noted that the following were possible purposes of evaluative activity or assessment in the 1950s:

1. Clarification and possible redefinition of the objectives of general education

2. Development of more adequate and reliable means of measurement

3. Appraisal of the development of students

4. Adaptation of courses and programs to the individual student

18

5. Motivation of student learning through continual self-evaluation

6. Improvement of instruction (p. 19)

Miller (1990) spoke to the general education debate that has never abated. This debate focuses on what general education should provide students and how this should be accomplished. Miller contended that defining general education has been a major challenge and likened the task to attempting to define beauty or love. "We all experience them but each of us responds in a different way" (p. 119). He further stated that the obtuse nature of general education predisposes it to a laundry list of definitions, and all of them are correct for one person or another. This disparity of perspective is a major reason why it is so difficult to come to a consensus on the best approach to assess the general education program. Nevertheless, institutions of higher learning have continued their quest, not only to define general education but also to set goals and determine which student-learning outcomes should be measured.

As general education programs grew and became more popular during the 1960s, 1970s, and 1980s, colleges and universities began to assess the value of what students learned and the effectiveness of the teaching in the 1980s and 1990s. Mayhew et al. (1990) noted, however, that curricular changes in general education programs have been slow. Charles Elliot, who fathered the course elective system in 1869, and Abbot Lowell, who established the distributive requirements system in 1909, initiated these changes. Students had a choice of subjects in which to enroll to meet their general education requirements based on their personal interest.

Mayhew et al. (1990) stressed that undergraduate education provided an opportunity for late adolescents to react to a variety of influences and stimuli that existed within society as they continued to develop a sense of their own values and attitudes. As discussions take place regarding the reformation movement within the general education arena, a new philosophy has emerged that supports students' devising their own degree programs based on their

socioeconomic background, cultural experiences, personal preferences, and long-term goals

(Mayhew et al.). Gaff (2003) stated that it was in the best interest of institutions of higher

learning to strengthen their general education programs in an effort to attract excellent students.

Another consequence of improving these programs was the enhancement of institutions'

reputations.

Quality in Higher Education

Lewis and Smith (1994) noted that beginning in the mid-1980s, many individuals in

higher education questioned the need for a revitalized focus on quality in higher education and

the applicability of quality concepts in the higher-education system. A review of the literature

indicates that there has been a significant surge of assessment activity within the higher-

education arena during the past forty years, both on the state level and at the institutional level.

The concern from approximately 1998 to the present has been whether assessment practitioners

have been measuring what is now deemed to be most important: student learning outcomes

(Chun, 2002).

There were four basic assessment approaches in higher education. They were categorized

as (a) actuarial data, (b) ratings of institutional quality, (c) student surveys, and (d) direct

measures of student learning (Chun, 2002).

According to Chun (2002), actuarial data provide

graduation rates, racial/ethnic composition of the student body, level of endowment,
student/faculty ratio, highest degree earned by faculty members, breadth and depth of
academic course offerings, selectivity ratio, admissions test scores of entering students,
and levels of external research funding. (p. 17)

20

The value of these kinds of data is the straightforwardness of the collection methods and the ease with which the data can be compared nationally.

On occasion, colleges and universities used actuarial data to assess institutional effectiveness (Chun, 2002). Chun noted, however, that when one used actuarial data, there was an assumption that a superior institution was associated with more and better resources (better funding, higher admissions grade-point averages, better faculty, and so forth). Examples of resources that were used for actuarial data were the National Center for Education Statistics and the Integrated Postsecondary Education Data System. Chun noted that although these databases included data (some data were from secondary sources) on student enrollment, faculty ranks, and institutional expenses, rarely did these objective data provide a reliable measure of student performance and achievement on learning outcomes.

Another assessment approach was based on rankings of institutional quality. An example of such a ranking was the *U. S. News & World Report*. Chun (2002) asserted that though the logic in the use of rankings was that so-called experts can best assess institutional quality, this journal came under harsh scrutiny over the years for several reasons. The paramount concern was the methods used to determine the rankings, including the methods used to calculate the rankings, the use of the information to make judgments about a broad range of institutions, and the subjective nature of the rankings. According to Chun,

> A 1977 report by the National Opinion Research Center (NORC)—commissioned by *U.S. News & World Report*—presented a systematic review of the methods used in the rankings. The NORC report notes that "the principal weaknesses of the current approach is that the weights used to combine the various measures into an overall rating lack any defensible empirical or theoretical basis…" The *U.S. News* weighting scheme is difficult to defend, and the NORC study concludes that, "since the method of combining measures is critical to the eventual ratings, the weights are the most vulnerable part of the methodology." (p. 18)

The truth of the matter is that even though rankings are not linked to data-driven evidence of student learning, rankings are still used by parents and students during the decision- making process regarding which institution to attend. According to Chun (2002), a study conducted by Monk and Ehrenberg for the National Bureau of Economic Research found that when an institution moves up one place in rankings, it results in an increase in admittance by .40 percent. The reality is that institutional rankings have a significant impact on potential students' behavior, on programmatic changes (in an effort to enhance the ranking of an institution) and in solidifying societal assumptions about what a quality undergraduate experience should be. Nevertheless, the literature suggests that there is no definable connection between rankings and student learning.

A third assessment approach, according to Chun (2002), was to measure institutional quality based on students' self reported satisfaction with support services, academic experiences, and future educational and career plans. In some scenarios, student surveys were supplemented with faculty, parent, alumni, and employer surveys. Examples of these surveys included the *Baccalaureate and Beyond Longitudinal Study* (based on the *National Postsecondary Student Aid Study*) and the *National Survey of Student Engagement*, used to measure students' participation in activities associated with learning and personal development (Kuh, 2003). Another example of a student survey used to collect data about an institution's effectiveness was the *Cooperative Institutional Research Program (CIRP) Survey* (Cooperative Institutional Research Program, n.d.). UCLA's Higher Education Research Institute administered this survey.

A primary criticism of the use of student surveys for an indication of quality was that of reliability. Because students were reporting their attitudes and feelings about a particular service or academic experience, this was not a direct measure of what students learned. Another

22

challenge associated with student surveys was reconciling students' self reports with what they actually achieved academically (Chun, 2002).

A fourth approach used to assess the quality of institutions of higher learning was to look closely at student learning. This strategy entailed determining what specific knowledge and skills were desirable for students to attain in order to be prepared for the workforce and for personal fulfillment after earning a four-year degree. Faculty and staff conducted most of the assessment work that relied on direct measures of student-learning outcomes with their students (Chun, 2002). A disadvantage of using locally developed measures of student learning was the inability to compare data across institutions. In view of this disadvantage, a more prevailing consideration was the use of direct measures of student-learning outcomes. They provided the most valuable data for curriculum reform and institutional evaluation (Banta et al., 1996; Huba & Freed, 2000; Palomba & Banta, 1999).

The need to renew and strengthen the focus on quality stemmed from several sources. Lewis and Smith (1994) found that the reasons for a change in attitude regarding the value of assessment included (a) reports and commentaries expressing distrust and dissatisfaction with the higher-education system initiated by public figures and society at large; (b) shifting trends of the student-body composition to older, married, and working individuals; (c) increased competition stemming from the demands of students for value-added education; (d) technological innovations and the reality of virtual campuses; (e) rising tuition costs; and (f) the reality of limited funding coupled with stakeholders' (legislators, parents, students) expectations of accomplishing more.

Lewis and Smith (1994) explained that although academicians may not have agreed with criticisms that were being voiced about the ineffectiveness and irrelevance of the current curriculum, little could be achieved by becoming defensive or closed-minded. The more

23

appropriate and beneficial reaction would be to embrace the philosophy of institutional

effectiveness, which includes annual assessment, program reviews, and strategic planning. A

consequence of embracing these processes is the continuous enhancement of the rich heritage

and viability of institutions of higher education (Seymour, 1993). Seymour added:

> Perhaps the greatest 'quality' problem that higher education faces is imbedded in the earlier story about the dean or professor who wanted to know "what does this have to do with me?" The intellectual center of a college campus is the academic programs, and at the heart of those programs are faculty members. Each faculty member, in turn, has her or his own transcendent definition of quality...The quality of their research is the degree to which they advance their discipline. The quality of their teaching is the degree to which they can impart that wisdom to others. (p. 48)

Stakeholders, such as parents and state legislators, were interested in an institution's

ability to retain and adequately prepare students for employers who were interested in hiring

competitive, high-caliber employees (Kuh, 2001; National Center for Postsecondary

Improvement, 2001). Not only were the benefits of educating students in the best way possible a

prime focus for those involved in institutional effectiveness, a superb academic environment also

played a major role in attracting gifts and grants to support facilities and faculty development.

These funds were especially needed for newly reformed programs and to support the redesign of

the curriculum (Gaff, 2003). According to Gaff (2003), "if attention to general education used to

be episodic, my sense is that it has become a sustained concern of most institutions" (p. i).

Ferren (2003) stated that even if a campus had the necessary resources to implement

changes in the general education curriculum, having necessary resources was not sufficient to be

successful. Students and faculty were also necessary factors in making changes. Without student

involvement and support for change, general education reform was difficult. Students tend to

view general education programs as a set of disconnected required courses that have little

significance to their career goals. If students do not gain a sense of the importance of the general

24

education program to their overall success, they make average-to-poor grades in these courses and, many times, are required to repeat them. Furthermore, a number of students take the dreaded required courses at a community college. Ferren reported that

> what students ask for in general education—passion, enthusiasm, and interest on the part of faculty—does not cost money. Even though students focus primarily on their job prospects and often claim internships are more important than art history, they do concede that the breadth of the general education program, when taught well, is good for them.

Controversy continued with regard to general education. The belief that students could achieve general education goals by simply taking a sampling of prescribed courses from a variety of disciplines was repeatedly challenged (Association of American Colleges and Universities [AACU], 1994). In the 1996 *Campus Trends Survey*, it was reported that 87% of the respondents reported introducing new general education requirements since 1985–86 and 76% reported an increase in the coherence of general education (Palomba & Banta, 1999). Gaff (2003) reported that in a survey administered in 2000, 57% of four-year institutions (including a significant number of Carnegie types) were undergoing an extensive evaluation of the core curriculum. Additionally, 64% of chief academic officers of those same institutions announced that there was an increased focus on the effectiveness of the general education program.

Faculty Engagement in Effective Assessment Strategies

As important as the appropriate choice of assessment methodology was to collecting meaningful data about learning and instructional delivery, Palomba and Banta (1999) maintained that a critical factor in the success of assessment activities was the extent to which the process engaged faculty. They stressed that "development of students' generic knowledge and skills is of interest to faculty in all disciplines. Knowledge of basic concepts in the fine arts, humanities,

25

social sciences, and natural sciences is fundamental to a deeper understanding of any field"

(p. 155). The role of the general education committee, which comprises faculty members, is to

create and enhance an engaging community across undergraduate programs to stimulate faculty-

member involvement (Gaff, 2003; Huba & Freed, 2000; Palomba & Banta, 1999). However, if

funding is unstable, then it is difficult to implement new ideas that might be of importance to

students and faculty (Kanter, Gamson, & London, 1997).

Romero (2001) stated that assigning the responsibility of developing standards for the

general education program to the state systems of higher education is not advisable. She

explained that the evolution of legislation for higher learning was based on frivolous incidents

that drove legislators to create standards that had not been appropriately founded.

Romero (2001) stressed the importance of engaging faculty in a comprehensive process.

She noted, "If faculty cannot embrace this role, they may lose the opportunity to influence the

results" (p. xiv).

Faculty should be involved in the planning and design of instruments, collection of

information, interpretation of results, and utilization of findings. It is important that cross-

discipline collaborations take place when developing strategies for assessment. Faculty and

academic administrators have to become more open and collaborative than ever before about

how they conduct the business of teaching and student learning (Angelo, 2002).

One particular concern, according to Palomba and Banta (1999), is that faculty members

who are involved in the assessment process for general education programs are based in different

academic departments and represent distinctly different disciplines. In their view, "almost all

successful programs to assess general education are led by strong interdisciplinary committees

that include faculty from across campus. Ordinarily, these committees select the approach to

26

assessment, evaluate information, and issue recommendations" (p. 241). Gaff (2003) affirmed

that his work was

> more like a struggle against "original sin." It involves trying to overcome academic pride... the tendency of faculty to focus on their own discipline, research interests, and individual autonomy rather than on the most fundamental knowledge and skills their students need from a curriculum.

Educators agree that there are inherent benefits in interdisciplinary teaching within the

core curriculum; however, it has received minimal support (Abrahamson & Kimsey, 2002). It is

widely accepted that in order for general education program assessment to be effective,

institutions must embrace and foster the interdisciplinary assessment approach.

Assessment that Leads to Improvement

In the last decade, there was a tremendous amount of activity in general education

curriculum reform and assessment (Palomba, 2002). Huba and Freed (2000) and Banta et al.

(1996) reported that in 1992 the American Association of Higher Education (AAHE) established

nine principles of good practice for assessing student learning:

1. The assessment of student learning begins with educational values.

2. Assessment is most effective when it reflects an understanding of learning as

    multidimensional, integrated, and revealed in performance over time.

3. Assessment works best when the programs it seeks to improve have clear, explicitly

    stated purposes.

4. Assessment requires attention to outcomes but also and equally to the experiences that

    lead to those outcomes.

5. Assessment works best when it is ongoing, not episodic.

6. Assessment fosters wider improvement when representatives from across the educational community are involved.

7. Assessment makes a difference when it begins with issues of use and illuminates questions people really care about.

8. Assessment is most likely to lead to improvement when it is part of a larger set of conditions that promote change.

9. Through assessment, educators meet responsibilities to students and to the public. (Banta et al., 1996, p. 2)

Huba and Freed (2000) also reported that in 1994 the North Central Association— Commission on Institutions of Higher Education compiled a similar list. The Association is one of six regional institutional accrediting associations in the United States. Through its commissions, it accredits and thereby grants membership to educational institutions in the 19-state North Central region: Arkansas, Arizona, Colorado, Iowa, Illinois, Indiana, Kansas, Michigan, Minnesota, Missouri, North Dakota, Nebraska, Ohio, Oklahoma, New Mexico, South Dakota, Wisconsin, West Virginia, and Wyoming (North Central Association of Colleges and Schools Website, n.d.)

The following list was very similar to the list developed by the AAHE; however, cost effectiveness, the need to assess the assessment process itself, and the provision of feedback to students and the institution were added. The principles were

1. Meaningful assessment flows from the institution's mission.

2. Meaningful assessment has a conceptual framework.

3. Meaningful assessment has faculty ownership/responsibility.

4. Meaningful assessment has institution-wide support.

28

5. Meaningful assessment uses multiple measures.

6. Meaningful assessment provides feedback to students and the institution.

7. Meaningful assessment is cost-effective.

8. Meaningful assessment does not restrict or inhibit goals of access, equity, and diversity established by the institution.

9. Meaningful assessment leads to improvement.

10. Meaningful assessment includes a process for evaluating the assessment program.

(Huba & Freed, 2000)

Palomba and Banta (1999) asserted that

> much of the value of assessment comes from the systematic way it makes educators question, discuss, share, and observe. As a result, assessment contributes greatly to the understanding of what educators do and to the choices they make about future directions for their work. Although in many cases, as Hutchings and Marchese note, "the possibility of proving a cause-and-effect relationship between assessment and improved learning is likely to remain elusive." (pp. 328–329)

According to Hubbard (1993), three concepts increase the chances for successful implementation of continuous quality improvement principles in higher education. The principles of parsimony (sharply focused goals, clear definitions of quality, fewer administrative layers, and the distinction between the critical and the trivial), benchmarking (comparing against best practices), and customer satisfaction are essential to the continuous quality movement.

Cornesky, McCool, Burns, and Weber (1992) explained that concerning educators and higher-education administrators, it should be assumed that everyone wanted to do a good job and was willing to work within processes and systems that support quality. It then naturally followed that the focus should be on continuously improving those processes and systems. If this was the commitment, then one could expect not only better quality outcomes but increased productivity and efficiency as well.

29

A review of the literature revealed an accepted philosophy of assessment that must be followed in order to experience a high level of participation and acceptance of the importance of assessment, whether one was conducting assessment in the major or in general education. Hubbard (1993) noted that if institutions of higher learning are truly concerned with quality, they should place their emphasis on prevention and improvement, not on ranking and sorting. According to Hubbard, this concept, which could be adapted from the manufacturing industry's model of assessment, provides one of the most challenging and important lessons for educators.

Posovac and Carey (1997) described the improvement-based model of assessment for the higher-education service industry. They advanced the idea that "changes can be made in programs when discrepancies are noted between what is observed and what was planned, projected, or needed" (p. 27). When the objective of evaluation is to improve, and this is a primary concern in colleges and universities, weaknesses in courses and programs provide a place to effect positive change. Posovac and Carey further explained that

> the improvement focused model—we believe—best meets the criteria necessary for effective evaluation: serving the needs of stakeholders, providing valid information, and offering an alternative point of view to those doing the really hard work of serving program participants. To carry this off without threatening the staff is the most challenging aspect of program evaluation. (p. 27)

Banta (1993) explained that the overarching concern in higher education relative to the measurement and continuous improvement of quality is whether lasting changes can be made in higher education through the adaptation of techniques that are working in industry. Because the for-profit industry and business culture are so broadly different from the traditions of institutions of higher learning, it is difficult for faculty to embrace the value of assessment. Nevertheless, pressure from stakeholders continued to propel the quality movement at a rapid pace (Evenbeck & Kahn, 2001).

Principles of an Effective General Education Program

Gaff (1993) noted that institutions of higher learning on a national scale must determine the nature of their respective general education programs. These institutions must scrutinize their academic program offerings to students and identify the linkages between curriculum and desired outcomes. The mission statement of colleges and universities should incorporate the actual plan for the institution, not just a wish list.

Gaff (1993) asserted that to best serve the needs of parents and potential employers, collaboration is the solution. The administration must be fully aware of what is occurring on college campuses and serve as a conduit of information with other administrators and students. The shared information must be accurate and consistent so that the entire institution can work together toward common goals. According to Gaff, if the reality of the general education program does not align with the intended core student-learning outcomes, then to be effective, the program should be revamped.

The scope of the subject areas of general education programs includes, but is not limited to, reading, writing, mathematics, critical thinking, problem solving, global perspectives, information gathering, and values and attitudes (Brown & Glasner, 1999). Across the United States, these areas have been integrated into general education programs, and the responsibility of how to conduct assessment has been assigned to a general education committee. In order to keep up with the changing external and internal forces, this committee is usually charged with monitoring student performance and achievement. With data about student achievement and performance, the committee is in a position to provide leadership for necessary changes that need to be made in the curriculum and support services (Brown & Glasner, 1999; Gaff, 1999).

In its *Strong Foundations Report*, the Association of American Colleges and Universities

(1994) identified 12 principles for effective general education. A total of 17 institutions of higher

learning that had all made significant changes in their programs generated these principles. They

are separated into two sections:

Part I. Articulating a Compelling Vision for General Education

Strong general education programs
1. Explicitly answer the question, "What is the point of general education?"
2. Embody institutional mission
3. Continuously strive for educational coherence
4. Are self-consciously value-based and teach social responsibility
5. Attend carefully to student experience
6. Are consciously designed so that they will continue to evolve

Part II. Forming an Evolving Community Based upon a Vision of General Education

Strong general education programs
7. Require and foster academic community
8. Have strong faculty and administrative leadership
9. Cultivate substantial and enduring support from multiple constituencies
10. Ensure continuing support for faculty, especially as they engage in dialogues across academic specialties
11. Reach beyond the classroom to the broad range of student co-curricular experiences
12. Assess and monitor progress toward an evolving vision through ongoing self-reflection

Weinstein and Van Mater Stone (1993) emphasized that when general education

programs focus only on knowledge enhancement, predictably, the programs are setting

themselves up for failure. This issue is particularly prevalent among students who are at risk for

academic failure or severe underachievement. This group of students requires options for

learning that extend beyond general knowledge and basic competencies in computation, reading,

and verbal and nonverbal communication. Traditional, longstanding general education programs

will not be valuable in preparing these students for lifelong learning nor in helping them to make

contributions to society.

To address the issue of obsolete general education programs, Weinstein and Van Mater Stone (1993) stated that students should participate in some form of assessment on entering college in order to gain additional knowledge about the preparation level of entering students. For example, students who register at the University of Texas complete a test that measures their learning and study strategies. This test (*Learning and Study Strategies Inventory* or *LASSI*) provides scores in ten different areas: "aptitude, motivation, time management, anxiety, concentration, information processing, selecting main ideas, study aids, self testing, and test strategies" (p. xxxviii).

Weinstein and Van Mater Stone (1993) also acknowledged that in this ever-changing global world, the future in education will be best served by faculty and administrators who understand that individuals who can identify their own learning needs and then tap the resources necessary to enhance appropriate learning experiences will be the most successful. Institutions of higher learning must "broaden their definitions of general education to include the development of self-regulated learners" (p. xxxviii).

Scholarship of General Education Assessment

Gaff (1999) documented that approximately 80 to 90% of the 1,600 member institutions (accredited colleges and universities) of the American Council on Education, reviewed or revised their undergraduate curriculum during the 1980s (S. Sanner, personal communication, May 22, 2003). Gaff (1999) reported that "reformers believed that by improving general education, the largest academic program on most campuses, they could have a significant impact upon the overall quality of baccalaureate education" (p. iii). Another indicator of the attention that has been given to general education is that AACU has assisted roughly 1,000 institutions in the reform of their general education programs.

Gaff (1999) noted that there was a major increase in the number of participants who attended conferences and institutes dedicated to providing assistance and knowledge about how to improve general education programs. This activity indicated that the need and desire of colleges and universities to revive and improve general education programs were pertinent to heightened quality in higher education.

The general education committee's role is to create and enhance an engaging community across undergraduate programs to stimulate faculty-member involvement (Gaff, 2003; Huba & Freed, 2000; Palomba & Banta, 1999). Nonetheless, if funding is unstable, then it is difficult to implement new ideas that may be of importance to students and faculty (Kanter et al., 1997).

Ferren (2003) contended that fiscal uncertainty negatively impacted reforms in general education curricula. Although there may be initial enthusiasm for change, this excitement can easily be dampened by budget cuts and a lack of resources. Ferren pointed out that "faculty generally play the primary role in designing the goals and structures of a new curriculum and leave it up to administrators to find the resources."

Gaff (2003) contended that there was always work to be done in improving general education programs. He further added that, "it is a constant challenge for the faculty as a whole to take responsibility for the curriculum as a whole. Engaging faculty understanding of and support for, general education is an unending task."

As an assessment scholar and practitioner, Maki (2002) emphasized that assessment of student learning normally surfaces as a critical process around the time of accreditation visits. She elucidated that although assessment has its roots in external mandates, institutions of higher

34

learning have had to evolve by identifying more meaningful internal reasons to conduct

assessment. In addition, she argued that

> the thread that connects faculty members' commitment to their work inside and outside
> of the classroom is intellectual curiosity—the characteristic ability to question, challenge,
> look at an issue from multiple perspectives, seek more information before rushing to
> judgment, raise questions, deliberate, and craft well-reasoned arguments. What faculty
> members exhibit themselves they also desire to instill in their students: They want to help
> create individuals who will question, challenge, view an issue from multiple perspectives,
> and, yes, wonder.

Maki (2002) stated that faculty's natural intellectual curiosity should serve as an impetus

for discovering connections between pedagogy and student learning. This type of discovery leads

to identification of best practices in teaching. Maki added that "rather than being disconnected

from content and teaching, assessment becomes the means of ascertaining what and how well

students achieve what faculty members intend them to achieve."

Maki (2003) noted that in the scholarship of the majors, faculty members depend on the

identification of replicated models to establish theories. According to Maki, it is the same in

measuring student-learning outcomes. Faculty members observe similar behaviors,

performances, and achievement to validate what students are able and unable to accomplish.

Defining Core Student-Learning Outcomes in General Education

Palomba (2001) noted that when faculty members developed learning-outcome

statements for general education, they were "describing the captured knowledge, skills and

values that graduates of an institution have in common" (p. xv). These skills are usually

transferable and are of importance to potential employers. Besides having a strong command of

the knowledge base in a major course of study, employers want to know what other skills

graduates gained and would bring to the workplace (Banta et al., 1996).

Siegel (2003) stated that because the range of possible outcomes for first-year programs is so broad, the range of outcomes that might be assessed is also extensive. The identification of specific outcomes to be assessed is closely tied to those who are involved in the assessment process and what they prescribe as a meaningful repertoire of outcomes. Because assessment meets requirements for the college, college accreditation bodies, program accreditation, and state mandates, the established learning outcomes tend to fall within the parameters of varied and sometimes unrelated needs.

Abrahamson and Kimsey (2002) reported that the general education committee at James Madison University (JMU) focused on an increasingly important question: How can the faculty best facilitate student learning in the area of creating knowledge out of the large body of available information and place that knowledge in its appropriate context? In response to this question, JMU developed a curriculum that transcended every major and professional program.

A distinct feature of JMU's revised general education program is the expectation that students would grasp a full understanding of how different disciplines view the world from their varied perspectives. It was successful in revitalizing its general education curriculum so that it meets the needs of the students, faculty, and employers (Abramson & Kimsey, 2002).

Interdisciplinary pedagogy was a primary catalyst for improving JMU's curriculum from the extremely compartmentalized curriculum to a more collaborative structure. The goal for this institution's general education program and for the majors and professional programs was to enhance all of the programs. A collaborative approach provided a conducive environment and sparked faculty engagement in providing a full and complete undergraduate education for students (Abrahamson & Kimsey, 2002).

Stone and Friedman (2002) gave an example of another collaborative effort used to energize the general education curriculum between faculty members. They stated that in 1990, in an effort to revitalize and focus the general education program, faculty members serving on the University Assessment Committee at the University of Wisconsin, Whitewater, developed a list of goals for students who would complete the general education program. These goals included

1. Think critically and analytically, integrate and synthesize knowledge, and draw conclusions from complex information

2. Make sound ethical and value judgments

3. Understand and appreciate the cultures of the U.S. and other countries, both contemporary and historical, appreciate cultural diversity, and live responsibly in an interdependent world

4. Acquire a base of knowledge common to educated persons

5. Communicate effectively in written, oral, and symbolic form with an appreciation of aesthetic and logical consideration in conveying ideas

6. Understand the natural and physical world

7. Appreciate the importance of the fine and performing arts

8. Develop the mathematical and quantitative skills necessary for calculation, analysis problem-solving, and the ability to use a computer

9. Understand the factors and habits that are essential for continual mental and physical health and well-being (pp. 201 and 202)

Palomba and Banta (1999) presented an example of reformation within the general education curriculum at Western Carolina University, which went through a major change in 1983. The system that was implemented in the restructuring project was a thematic model, rather

37

than a discipline-based one. The core curriculum was divided into two key areas—foundations and perspectives.

> Written communication; mathematics; computer literacy; leisure and fitness; and thinking, reasoning, and expression courses are classified as foundations courses. Within the perspectives area are courses in social sciences and contemporary institutions, physical and biological sciences, the humanities, fine and performing arts, comparative cultures, and the human past. In addition, all general education courses [were] required to incorporate instruction and/or practice in seven skills defined in detail by the faculty. The skills are the use of written communication, oral communication, critical thinking, logical reasoning, references and resources, the scientific method, and the process of valuing. The General Education Committee, reporting to the Council on Instruction and Curriculum of the faculty senate, is charged to monitor and assess the general education curriculum. (p. 157)

An Assessment Task Force on the Core Curriculum was established at Santa Clara University to develop, in collaboration with other key faculty members, statements of intended core learning outcomes for general education goals that had been defined. Six groups were organized to plan and institute a pilot assessment project for each core goal (Palomba & Banta, 1999).

According to Palomba and Banta (1999), the immediate objective during the first year of this pilot program was to design a curriculum for critical writing, ethics, ethnic/women's studies, mathematics, religious studies, and the western culture sequence. A strong message was delivered to the faculty that accentuated the purpose of the pilot program: "not program evaluation but inquiry and dialogue about curricular goals and learning outcomes" (p. 160).

Outcome statements for the six groups included language that articulated what students should know and be able to do at the conclusion of the general education program. For mathematics, students would be able to identify skills in logical reasoning and translation of mathematical ideas. Students would also be able to appreciate the uses of mathematics. The ethics subgroup articulated four outcomes, but in reality assessed only moral reasoning. The ethnic/women's studies group identified appropriate recognition of and understanding of varied experiences and the ability to prioritize the idea of inclusiveness in society. The writing group chose skills in grammar and vocabulary and successful completion of the articulation and development of an original thesis (Palomba & Banta, 1999).

Another popular thematic area of general education is diversity. Humphreys (1997) noted that in the area of diversity, many campuses strove to establish clear, concise learning goals for diversity courses. Included in the goals was the idea of developing skills to function in a diverse world where students recognized the role of varied backgrounds and influences on political, civic, and cross-cultural decision-making. A specific student-learning outcome at North Seattle Community College for the diversity requirement within the general education curriculum required that students learn how "to deal constructively with information, ideas, and emotions associated with diversity and conflict" (p. 22).

The Learning Process

Benjamin Bloom worked as the leader of a group of educational psychologists in 1956. The task that they undertook was the development of a classification of the levels of intellectual behavior that are crucial to the learning process. This classification became a taxonomy that included three overlapping domains: cognitive, affective, and psychomotor (Lane, n.d.). (See Table 1.)

Table 1

Types and Levels of Learning (Bloom's Taxonomy)

Categories	Types and levels of learning
Cognitive	
	recall and intellectual levels
	knowledge
	comprehension
	application
	analysis
	synthesis
	evaluation
Affective	
	attitudes
	values
	interests
	appreciation and feelings towards people, ideas, places, and objects
Psychomotor skills	
	perception
	guided responses
	mechanical
	complex responses
	adaptation
	origination

Cognitive learning requires the skill of recall and the intellectual skills of comprehension, organization, analysis and synthesis of data, application of knowledge, choice among alternatives in solving problems, and evaluation of ideas and actions. Affective learning is indicated by behaviors, which demonstrate attitudes such as awareness, involvement, engagement, and the ability to listen and respond. Psychomotor learning is manifested by physical abilities (e.g., coordination, dexterity, manipulation, endurance, swiftness, fine-motor capabilities) (Lane, n.d.).

The Center for Education (2001) provided an update report on the progress that has been made in the sciences of thinking and learning. The report described the research in the following terms:

> In the latter part of the 20th century, study of the human mind generated considerable insight into one of the most powerful questions of science: How do people think and learn? Evidence from a variety of disciplines—cognitive psychology, developmental psychology, computer science, anthropology, linguistics, and neuroscience, in particular—has advanced our understanding of such matters as how knowledge is organized in the mind; how children develop conceptual understanding; how people acquire expertise in specific subjects and domains of work; how participation in various forms of practice and community shapes understanding; and what happens in the physical structures of the brain during the processes of learning, storing, and retrieving information. (p. 59)

Maki (2003) and Huba and Freed (2000) explained that it is critical for assessment practitioners to be aware of all of the aspects of learning and how students' experiences play a major role in what they ultimately will be able to know, think, and do. Siegel (2003) noted that research showed that the quality of effort by students in preparing themselves is one of the primary indicators of how successful they would be in college. In other words, background and demographics are not as important as the experiences that students have while in college.

If students are determined to learn what is needed in order to prepare themselves for the workforce and colleges provide these agreed-upon experiences, then students will most likely be successful in achieving the desired learning outcomes. Kuh (2003) asserted that just because a particular course is offered and required by the college, one should not conclude that this leads to automatic student success. It is critical for students to be engaged in the process in more than one way (e.g., faculty interaction, tutoring centers, mentors) in order to have a level of achievement that matters.

Methods of Assessment: Identification of Effective Measurement Approaches

The Center for Education (2001) stated that all assessment is based on a concept that underlies the process by which people learn, what people know, and how knowledge and understanding are related. The foundations of each measurement approach are certain beliefs about the types of performances that are necessary in order to gain information about the level of understanding and attitudinal positions students hold. Finally, each assessment approach is based on an established assumption about how to analyze the data in an effort to make appropriate changes to enhance students' performance, achievement, and ultimate integration into and long-term success in the workplace.

The foundations influence all aspects of an assessment's design and use, including content, format, scoring, reporting, and use of the results. Even though these fundamental principles are sometimes more implicit than explicit, they are still influential. In fact, it is often the tacit nature of the foundations and the failure to question basic assumptions that create conflicts about the meaning and value of assessment results (Center for Education, 2001). Advances in the study of thinking and learning (cognitive science) and in the field of measurement (psychometrics) stimulated people to think in new ways about how students learn and what they know, what is therefore worth assessing, and how to obtain useful information about student competencies (Center for Education, 2001).

Maki (2003) asserted that institutions of higher learning would be effective in enhancing student learning if they aligned "pedagogy, curricular and co-curricular design (sequence), instructional design, educational practices, such as learning communities, educational tools, students' learning histories/styles and methods to capture learning" (p. ii). When assessment practitioners embarked on collecting data about student learning, they were interested in learning about knowledge that led to understanding, abilities and attitudes, values, and dispositions.

Stone and Friedman (2002) posited that although there is a growing consensus about the importance of a coherent general education curriculum in post-secondary institutions,

> little progress has been made in determining if students are learning what they are supposed to be learning in such courses. Despite a remarkable increase in commitment to assessment over the past 15 years ... assessment of general education lags far behind. (pp. 199, 200)

Stone and Friedman (2002) continued to detail reasons why assessment of general education programs have not been embraced comprehensively. It appears that many institutions, even those under pressure by stakeholders, have still not bought into the value of assessment. Approximately 25% of all institutions of higher learning have no assessment criteria or process and do not intend to begin the assessment effort.

Some institutions redesigned and instituted a superior general education curriculum but did not developed a plan for assessing the student-learning outcomes associated with the curriculum. According to Stone and Friedman (2002), non-traditional approaches for assessment need to be considered by those individuals responsible for assessment. They concluded that general education does not happen separate from the assessment of the majors. Assessment of general education is impacted greatly by external and internal forces. In conjunction with assessing disciplines' learning outcomes, one could measure general education student learning outcomes specifically related to students' overall development (verbal skills, quantitative skills, reasoning skills, ability to appreciate others' culture, etc.). These outcomes could be and should be practiced and developed on a continuous basis in the major until graduation assessment.

According to Palomba and Banta (1999), of particular concern is that faculty members involved in the assessment process for general education programs are based in different

43

academic departments and represent different disciplines. They contended that in order for an assessment initiative to be effective, it must integrate strong interdisciplinary committees across the institution. These committees are typically responsible for determining which student learning outcomes should be assessed, selecting the assessment methods, and providing feedback to improve the process. This approach emphasizes a more integrated model of assessment that takes into account not only specific knowledge for a given field of study but the assessment of interdisciplinary studies as well as general education courses.

Various unconventional assessment approaches yield much more reliable and valid data. These nontraditional approaches also reduce the likelihood that a single measure is used, which could result in low-integrity data (Banta et al., 1996; Pike, 2002).

Recent work in the state systems in Georgia and Utah addressed the issue of linking assessment to shared goals. Schoenberg (2001) indicated that

> during the 1998–99 academic year, faculty from these states' public two- and four-year institutions began working with AAC&U (supported by a grant from the U.S. Department of Education's Fund for the Improvement of Postsecondary Education) to develop new system-wide goals for general education, to gain broad faculty and student understanding of them, and to come up with ways to assess them. (p. 5)

Siegel (2003) stated that the assessment of student outcomes makes use of a combination of survey instruments, questionnaires, qualitative approaches, and other methods of data collection. The surveys are best grouped based on their function and purpose. Included in the diverse approaches of measuring student-learning outcomes and perceptions are surveys (pre-enrollment and baseline); standardized placement and knowledge surveys; post survey (after the first year or after the general education program had been completed); surveys measuring students' attitudes, behaviors, perception of skills, satisfaction, and behavior; and locally developed surveys designed to measure students' perceptions of a specific college campus. Other

44

assessment methods include focus groups, analysis of syllabi, embedded course questions, essays using rubrics, portfolios (including web-based portfolios), advisory boards, and panels to judge student performance.

Palomba and Banta (1999) explained that although program-level assessment is crucial, it is also imperative that campus-wide assessment efforts gain a level of importance as well. "When planned by faculty, staff, and students who represent a broad cross-section of the campus and when results are communicated in meaningful ways, these activities help campus units see what they have in common as an institution" (p. 342).

Examples of campus-wide assessment include graduating-senior surveys, alumni surveys, and writing-competence examinations. Data from these methods of assessment can provide useful information when analyzed aggregately; however, they can provide more specific knowledge about students, employers, parents, and so on when disaggregated (Palomba & Banta, 1999).

Typically, faculty-based committees comprise professors from a variety of disciplines who are responsible for curriculum design (courses to be taught and the sequence of courses), planning, and teaching and learning assessment strategies (Angelo, 2002). Miller (1990) stressed that "no one being 'in charge' of the campus general education program can be a serious weakness" (p.127).

According to Bauer and Frawley (2002), within undergraduate studies, a clear, concise assessment plan must be based on an understanding of the institution's goals for general education and how those goals fit into the mission of the institution. Additionally, faculty and other planners must be aware of how general education is merged into the curriculum and co-curriculum and how appropriate assessment methods can be effective in light of the vast differences among institutions' students and programs.

Palomba (2002) called attention to the scholarly works of many assessment practitioners who have reached a consensus about meaningful methods of assessment. Examples of these ways of collecting assessment data include performance evaluation and capstone experiences.

Although locally developed and nationally normed objective tests continue to be used to assess student learning, institutions of higher learning are increasingly implementing performance evaluations (e.g., papers, exhibits, demonstrations) to assess students' level of understanding of substantive knowledge and specialized skills that are expected (Ewell, 2001; Maki, 2001). Additionally, students, through self-evaluation and self-reporting, provide data about their attitudes about the learning environment (Huba and Freed, 2000; Palomba and Banta, 1999).

Capstone assessment is an opportune way to allow seniors to give an indication about their grasp of broad or core learning outcomes and proficiency in general education goals (Palomba, 2002; Palomba & Banta, 1999). Palomba and Banta reported that at Southern Illinois University, Edwardsville, the Senior Assignment is an assessment tool that provides an opportunity for seniors to engage in a scholarly activity that was supervised by a professor. The culminating product of this assignment can be in the form of a thesis, poster, presentation, design, or other substantiation that allows a set of courses to be assessed.

Portfolios are fast becoming a viable method of assessment for many colleges and universities. The use of portfolios to assess student-learning outcomes in the general education area is particularly useful because of diversity in the repertoire of student-learning outcomes (Palomba & Banta, 1999; Pike, 2001). Students select examples of their classroom work and

46

assignments and enter them either manually (a folder) or electronically (web-based or on a disc) to be reviewed by a panel. A rubric that is understood and used by the faculty who are involved in the portfolio process is used to assess the work that is included in a portfolio (Palomba & Banta, 1999).

Banta et al. (1996) shared a case study portraying Northeast Missouri State University in its use of portfolios as a local complementary tool for assessment of its liberal arts and sciences core curriculum (used in conjunction with standardized tests and student satisfaction surveys). Northeast Missouri State University is a Master's I, Public institution with an enrollment of 6,200 students. Students participated in an orientation at the beginning of their freshmen year. In this orientation, they were introduced to the idea of a portfolio and the purpose and scope of the assessment tool. It was explained to them that they would compile a collection of their work during their senior year. During specified times of the year, more information about the portfolios was made available.

This assessment approach was an opportunity for students to showcase their actual work and provided data about their achievement and performance in areas of critical thinking, interdisciplinary synthesis, scientific and mathematical reasoning, aesthetic appreciation, and co-curricular learning. Faculty members were required to identify a specific assignment or project from each course to be included in the portfolio and also to develop the criteria for the senior portfolios. Throughout the year advisers discussed and reviewed the specific work that should be maintained in the portfolio. Students were kept apprised of the material that they should archive to be reviewed during the senior year (Banta et al., 1996).

During the senior year, faculty members met with the appropriate students and, in more detail, discussed what the expectations were for the portfolio at the end of the senior year.

47

Students were required to make copies (at the institution's expense) and submit the collection of work for review by twenty faculty members, who were paid a stipend of $500 to participate in the entire reading and review process (Banta et al., 1996). Typically, faculty members were reluctant to participate in this assessment activity, but at the conclusion of the task found the experience rewarding. According to Banta et al., this experience provided faculty members with a more enhanced picture of student learning and the impact that the university had on students than any other faculty-driven activity.

Banta et al. (1996) presented another case study that was conducted at Western Carolina University, which is a Master's I, Public institution with approximately 6,300 students enrolled. This institution decided to use focus groups after the determination was made to revitalize the general education program. The General Education Committee mapped a process of program review that supported a systematic evaluation of the general education areas within a three-year span. This process reviewed the results of a myriad of assessment methods to evaluate courses in each of the eleven areas of study to provide feedback to the focus groups and to the departments offering courses within the area. Faculty members served in focus groups and were charged with exchanging ideas about the commonalities among courses in each thematic area and the development of educational goals. They were also responsible for deciding on the methods of measuring for each of the eleven areas of general education. After the focus groups reported their plan to the General Education Committee, a foundation was laid for continuous improvement within the program.

When this process began, faculty members were not overly enthusiastic about being integrally involved with assessing student learning in the general education program. It was not clear to them what skills should be assessed. However, once the General Education Committee defined the skills and the most basic level of instruction and practice required for each skill, the faculty felt that they were in a much better position to move forward in the process (Banta et al., 1996). The focus group found it challenging to agree on a set of common goals for the thinking, reasoning, and expression courses. Ultimately, it was recommended, after examining the students' needs, that this foundation area be changed to oral communication. This change was the initial change made in the curriculum and was the first change since 1984. It was evident that this change was the result of an effective review process, as the faculty members that were making the recommendations were removing their own courses.

Palomba and Banta (1999) explained that measures in assessment used at Santa Clara University during its pilot assessment project (discussed in the earlier section on Defining Core Student Learning Outcomes in General Education) included

> essays rated on scoring criteria developed for this project (writing and ethnic/women's studies), a questionnaire and short skills examination (mathematics), an audiotaped class discussion of freedom and equality (Western culture), an audiotaped focus group on the religious dimensions of students' SCU education (religious studies), and an abbreviated version of the Defining Issues Test (DIT) to assess moral reasoning (ethics). (p. 161)

The Rand Corporation's Council for Aid to Education (CAE) recently undertook a project to build an alternative assessment approach for higher education. Benjamin and Chun (2003) noted that this approach, which measured the 'value added' by an institution, grew into the Collegiate Learning Assessment (CLA) project. After they conducted a feasibility study in 2002 with more than 1,300 students at 14 colleges and universities, they found the approach to be viable and effective.

The CLA project was a change from traditional assessment methods in four distinct ways. First, it used direct assessment measures of student learning instead of indirect measures (e.g., entrance examinations, student self-assessments, faculty perceptions from surveys). Second, the

49

CLA project measured general education skills (e.g., critical thinking, reasoning, communication) vs. discipline content. Third, the approach for measuring used a sample method instead of a census (Benjamin & Chun, 2003). Various intended outcomes were measured using samples of the student population. A matrix was developed, which exhibited performance of samples of students across the curriculum. Finally, the project's goal was to assess value added (what the institution had contributed to student development and learning). The measures of value added were established in the following ways:

> (1) We measure how well an institution's students perform relative to "similarly situated" students (defined in terms of their SAT or ACT scores), and (2) we measure how much students' skills improve during the tenure at the institution through a pre-test/post-test model. (Benjamin & Chun, 2003)

Walvoord and Anderson (1998) contended that in order to assess general education outcomes, one must define the outcomes but not spend an extensive amount of time trying to get everyone across the entire campus to agree with the definition. Additionally, faculty should be amenable to nontraditional approaches to assessment (assessment methods outside of standardized tests). Walvoord and Anderson also stressed that a mission statement for general education may need to be simplified in order to identify meaningful measurement approaches.

The classroom-based assessment method was recommended strongly by Walvoord during a workshop that she facilitated in 1998 at Raymond Walters College. She suggested that faculty use classroom tests and exam scores to answer questions about student performance. According to Walvoord, the faculty who participated in the workshop responded well to this measurement approach (Walvoord & Anderson, 1998).

Ferren (2003) and Muffo (2001) emphasized the importance of assessing general education programs. It was noted that most colleges and universities included general education as an integral part of their undergraduate curricula. The knowledge, skills, behaviors, and

50

attitudes that were considered desirable for successful college graduates were emphasized across academic disciplines and departments. Although the pedagogical approaches and teaching strategies may have been vastly different from one institution to the next, the core intended learning outcomes were closely aligned. However, it was becoming increasingly apparent, according to Ferren, that there were scarce tools available for systemic assessment of general education goals.

Ferren (2003) noted that individual courses were much easier to assess than general education because general education was not so neatly separated into its own discipline. Typically, tools that assessed recall were used to measure learning outcomes for specific disciplines; however, general education assessment was unique in that it was concerned with how well students demonstrated their ability to use information. Measurement approaches that relied on using tools that measure students' recall aptitude were not appropriate for measuring general education learning outcomes.

Improving the General Education Program Through the Use of Assessment Results

Maki (2002) commented on the meaningful implementation of assessment within institutions of higher learning for the purpose of improvement:

> Creating an institutional environment that fosters inquiry into student learning means redesigning or creating new structures and processes to allow significant time for faculty and other educational professionals to conduct research on student learning, interpret results of assessment, and reflect on these interpretations to advance innovations in teaching and curricular design.

> Institutions that claim assessment as their own will likely transform themselves to sustain a focus on student learning. The faculty will be supported by institutional structures, processes, and communication channels that symbolize the integration of assessment of student learning into the rhythms of institutional life. Time and space for discourse that focuses on the results of assessment—that builds in periods of self-reflection about students' achievement of programmatic and institutional outcomes, as well as about

innovations in pedagogy and curriculum—will mark institutional commitment to student learning. (p. iv)

Huba and Freed (2000) and Palomba and Banta (1999) discussed aspects of assessment that should include assessing the process itself. A fundamental area that needs improvement is the actual process that is being used to assess learning outcomes. Elements such as important constituency identification, clear statements of learning outcomes, alignment of assessment methods with goals, and the use of results in the curriculum and budget decision-making process should all be monitored. Much of the learning that takes place during an assessment process is about the assessment process itself.

Grob and Kuehl (1997) acknowledged that though it is difficult in a comprehensive university to require that every student across the institution complete identical courses, it is worth the effort to develop a common core curriculum. Fairleigh Dickinson University is a comprehensive multicampus institution that instituted such a program. Students are required to complete a sequence of four courses beginning in the second semester of their freshmen year. The sequence ends in the first semester of their junior year. The courses range from reflections on individuality (Perspectives on the Individual) to themes of freedom and equality (The American Experience).

Before this program was instituted, a campus-wide assessment was conducted to determine the attitude of students and faculty regarding the general education program. This assessment resulted in several key findings, which served to establish the foundation for change. Some of the changes that were discussed and eventually implemented included a) making the program more coherent, b) making texts available that are produced by the program (in-house publications of readings), c) alerting students to connections among themes and questions, and d) developing writing assignments that required students to use knowledge from past courses (Grob & Kuehl, 1997).

One significant change that occurred in implementing faculty-owned assessment activities at Western Carolina University was in the perceptions of faculty and students concerning the process. Faculty realized that assessment was important and that it was a meaningful tool for determining what students were learning and what they were not learning (Palomba & Banta, 1999). Another change, according to Palomba and Banta, and a second type of improvement, was the increased level of information about the general education program. An example of the type of information that was obtained was the development of specific definitions of the seven skills that were agreed on by the faculty senate and the chancellor. The defined skills enabled the assessment team to determine the extent to which the outcomes were being taught and a sense for what students should know, think, or do. A third category of improvement was the added dimension of coherence across the curriculum.

Palomba and Banta (1999) described the types of changes that benefited Santa Clara University after the inception of their pilot assessment project.

> The project's focus on description of learning outcomes generated useful discussion among task force members and the many faculty they interviewed to help them clarify curricular goals...First, we learned that faculty become quite engaged in serious inquiry about learning outcomes; the most productive conversations occurred in the context of developing outcome statements and devising and applying criteria for evaluating essays. Second, we reaffirmed that assessment requires a great deal of work! Technical and clerical support from the dean's office was essential for timely completion of these projects. We also learned that few students are tempted by mailed invitations even when generous incentives and flexible scheduling are offered. (A methodology we plan to try in the future is to offer chances for a drawing to win a more substantial prize.) We obtained much better results using course-embedded methodologies: asking faculty to administer questionnaires in class (ethics); using assignments already planned by faculty (writing and ethnic/women's studies). And we found that developing our own measures and criteria yields far greater engagement in the process and interest in the results than choosing existing measures for convenience. (p. 162)

53

Seymour (1993) contended that quality was not a moment in time; the idea that you reach an ultimate goal and can maintain the status quo was not acceptable. Seymour stressed the importance of the idea of continuous improvement. He said that "quality is an eternal struggle… 'good enough' is simply not good enough. There is always a better way, a simpler approach, a more elegant solution" (p. 15).

Conclusion

It is evident that general education serves an important purpose in the education of students pursuing knowledge and skills. As attitudes are formed about the world in which they live, students are guided and shaped through their experiences in colleges and universities across the country.

Quality is an important aspect of higher education, specifically as it relates to general education. Faculty's leadership and continual involvement in general education assessment are two critical factors in the overall success of the level of quality of the core curriculum.

As assessment practitioners strive to improve assessment approaches and methodologies, implementation of a scholarship of assessment has become imperative. Assessment that leads to improvement is the focus of institutions across the United States, as they identify meaningful student-learning outcomes and evaluate how well students are doing in the areas of what they should know, think, and do.

CHAPTER 3

RESEARCH DESIGN AND METHODOLOGY

This study was initiated in the Fall Semester 2003. The final analysis and conclusions were completed and presented in Spring 2004. This chapter describes the research design, instrument design, setting, population of the study, data collection, and analysis of the data.

Research Design

Having selected an area of study—general education assessment—the researcher was faced with a decision concerning choice of instrument to carry out the study. A quantitative instrument seemed a reasonable choice at first, but after a brief review of the literature, it was clear that there was not enough knowledge available about general education assessment to justify conducting a quantitative research study.

Creswell (1998) asserted that a qualitative study that takes a grounded theory approach seeks to generate or discover a theory. According to Creswell "the centerpiece of grounded theory research is the development or generation of a theory closely related to the context of the phenomenon being studied" (p. 56). A theory is a warranted relationship among concepts and sets of concepts. This theory is clearly described by the researcher at the conclusion of the study in the form of a narrative statement, a visual picture, or a series of hypotheses or propositions.

Creswell (1998) further stated that there are strong reasons for engaging in qualitative research versus quantitative research. Among these, the nature of the research question (how or what, in contrast to why in quantitative studies) is conducive to a qualitative study. Second, the topic needs to be explored (variables are not easily known). Third, a qualitative study provides a detailed picture of the topic. Fourth, there is a distinct benefit in studying participants in their natural environment. Fifth, the prospective readers of the research would gain from qualitative research as compared to quantitative research. Sixth, the researcher is in a learning mode and will benefit from what is learned through the research and can then tell the story from the participant's perspective rather than as an expert passing judgment.

Morse and Richards (2002) noted that qualitative data come from various sources, including documents, interviews, field notes, and observations. Researchers may use a myriad of methods to analyze data; however, each method should have integrity and result in new understanding and theories about the data. The results should also provide rich descriptions, a theory to be tested later with quantitative research, or a qualitatively developed theory that can be used.

Morse and Richards (2002) stated that qualitative studies are appropriate when trying to determine "What is going on here?" or "How are we doing with this innovation?" (p. xxxix). Miles and Huberman (1994) and Patten (2000) described qualitative analysis as powerful, and they noted that this type of research is an excellent research approach for discovery, exploring a new area, and developing a hypothesis. Morse and Richards (2002) noted that "making data" is a collaborative, continual process "in which data are interactively negotiated by the researcher and participants; the data are rarely fixed and unchanging, never exactly replicating what is being studied" (p. 87).

Once the decision was made to conduct a qualitative study, the researcher reviewed the literature about the methodologies used in qualitative studies and investigated three grounded

56

theory models—positivist, postmodernist, and constructivist—and chose the model developed by Strauss and Corbin (1990, 1997, 1998).

According to Strauss and Corbin (1998), grounded theory methods focus on analytic strategies, not data collection approaches. The original grounded theory approach embraced traditional positivism, with its assumptions of an objective, external reality; a neutral observer who discovered data; reductionist inquiry of manageable research problems; and objectivist rendering of data.

Strauss and Corbin (1997, 1998) assumed an objective external reality underpinning, aimed at unbiased data collection and a set of technical procedures and verification of those procedures. Their post-positivist model gives a voice to the respondents and takes every measure to represent them as accurately as possible. The focus is on discovering something and acknowledging how this something is executed. The results and findings of the study are displayed in visuals representing the facts, a rich description of overt data, and conditional statements.

This study used the Strauss and Corbin (1990, 1997, 1998) model of grounded theory. The three major elements of qualitative research data are (a) data from various sources, (b) procedures used to interpret and organize data, and (c) writing or orally presenting the results of the study.

This approach required the researcher to be objective in the data collection phase. It also assumed that a set of technical procedures and verification of those procedures were closely adhered to. Another characteristic of Strauss and Corbin's (1990, 1997, 1998) version of the grounded theory approach was that respondents had a voice in the final analysis and that accuracy was essential. Finally, the findings were represented as rich descriptions of data, the proposition of a theory, and conditional statements.

Strauss and Corbin (1998) noted that "if theory building is indeed the goal of a research project, then findings should be presented as a set of interrelated concepts, not just a listing of themes" (p. 145). Relational statements, like concepts, are abstracted from the data. However, because they are interpreted abstractions and not the descriptive details of each case (raw data), they (like concepts) are "constructed" out of data by the analyst. Miles and Huberman (1994) stressed that in some cases, research could ultimately contribute to further development and refinement of existing concepts in the field.

The theoretical framework explains a relevant educational phenomenon. The statements of relationship delineates who, what, where, why, how, and what consequences or event occurs. According to Strauss and Corbin (1990, 1998) and Miles and Huberman (1994), after the researcher has related concepts through statements of relationship into a clear frame, the researcher may then develop a theory (p. 22).

Unlike theories that may be derived from quantitative studies, the theory that emerges from qualitative studies cannot be generalized. However, the theory may lead to more focused qualitative studies (theoretical sampling) in the same area and to quantitative studies (Strauss & Corbin, 1990, 1998).

Grounded theory provides researchers with the analytic tools to develop theoretical statements using a systematic approach.

Analytic Tools Used in Grounded Theory

Three primary analytic tools are used to analyze the data in this study: open coding, axial coding, and selective coding (Strauss & Corbin, 1998).

1. Open coding opens up the text and reveals thoughts, ideas, and meanings. If this first analytic step is not done, the rest of the analysis could not be executed. Data are broken down into small parts, scrutinized, and compared for similarities and differences. Events, things, and actions/interactions that are found to be similar in nature or connected in meaning are clustered under more abstract concepts termed "categories."

2. Axial coding links categories to their subcategories at the level of properties and dimensions.

3. Selective coding integrates and refines the theory.

The term axial is used because the coding is done around the axis of a particular category. For example, the category "purpose" was linked to the subcategory "knowledge," because one of the reasons that the core curriculum is offered is to impart knowledge. The other three subcategories were skills, behaviors, and beliefs and values. This step is the "act of relating categories to subcategories along the lines of their properties and dimensions" (Strauss & Corbin, 1990). This level of coding is used to answer questions such as why, how, how come, where, when, and with what results. This stage of analysis aids the researcher in determining properties of the categories and dimensions. For example, if someone were conducting a study on movement from one place to another, flight might be one of the categories. The properties of flight might be height, speed, and the duration of the flight. Identifying how high and how fast could further contextualize the properties and determine how long something can fly. Birds fly lower, slower, and for shorter distances than do planes. Axial coding served to reassemble data that had been dissected during open coding. See Table 2 for analytic tools.

Table 2

Analytic Tools of Grounded Theory

Types of Coding	Explanation
Open Coding	Opens up the text and reveal thoughts ideas and meanings. If this first analytic step is not done, the rest of the analysis could not be executed.
	Breaks down data into small parts, scrutinizes data, and compares data for similarities and differences.
Axial Coding	Connects categories with subcategories.
	Makes connections between categories and its subcategories.
	Codes conditions that give rise to the category, its context, the social interactions through which it is handled, and its consequences. (This can be done during initial coding.)
Selective Coding	Integrates and refines the theory.
Other Tools	Memos: Records thoughts about the data during analysis.
	Diagrams: Develops visual pictures of concepts, relationships, and interrelationships

Memos and diagrams provided important tools for analysis. The researcher used memos to record thoughts and interpretations, questions, and future plans for analysis throughout the study. Diagramming created a visual picture of the concepts that emerged throughout the analysis.

Following is a summary of the benefits of coding (Charmaz, 2000):

1. Steers the researcher away from the literature and personal experience

2. Keeps researcher from traditional ways of thinking about concepts and ideas

3. Stimulates the inductive process

4. Concentrates on the data and does not overlook anything

5. Stays tuned in to what respondents are saying and doing

6. Avoids overlooking key concepts

7. Ensures that important questions are asked and answers are provided

8. Ensures that labeling of concepts is meaningful

9. Identifies properties and dimensions or categories or themes

<u>Instrument Design</u>

The researcher developed a survey based on a review of the literature. The survey was approved by the IRB (Appendix H). The survey included a cover letter (see Appendix B), which introduced the purpose of the study and provided instructions to potential respondents. The instructions included information applicable to the hard-copy version of the instrument and to the web-based version. The URL for the web-based version was provided along with suggestions for saving a draft of responses in a Word or equivalent document until the respondent was ready to submit the web-based questionnaire.

Following are the six questions presented in the survey (see Table 3; see Appendix F):

S1. Briefly provide a description of the purpose of your general education program.

S2. What core general education student-learning outcomes have been developed and are being measured at your institution (for example, the ability to think critically, the ability to communicate effectively both written and verbal, the ability to solve quantitative problems)?

S3. What types of measurement approaches (instruments, data-collection methods) are being used to assess these core student-learning outcomes at your institution (for example, portfolios, standardized tests, essays, embedded test questions)?

S4. Which core student-learning outcome measurement instruments and data-collection methods have yielded the type of data that has made it possible to make changes in your general education program, including curricula changes, specific course revisions, teaching strategies, etc.?

S5. Describe improvements that have been made at your institutions as a result of data collected from core student-learning outcomes assessment (for example, revised course content, revised curriculum, different delivery of instruction).

S6. As you assess your General Education Program and analyze the results, have you learned that there are some positive things that you are doing that are effective in the program? If yes, briefly describe those positive strategies.

Table 3

Research Questions With Survey Questions

Research Questions	Survey Questions
R1. What core general education student-learning outcomes are being assessed at urban and metropolitan colleges and universities? R4. What differences, if any, exist in the institutions' stated intended core student-learning outcomes based on the type (four-year and graduate level) and size of the institution?	S2. What core general education student-learning outcomes have been developed and are being measured at your institution? For example, the ability to think critically, the ability to communicate effectively both written and verbal, the ability to solve quantitative problems, etc.
R2. What instruments and methods of data collection are being used to assess core general education student-learning outcomes at urban and metropolitan universities?	S3. What types of measurement approaches (instruments, data collection methods) are being used to assess these core student-learning outcomes at your institution? For example, portfolios, standardized tests, essays, embedded test questions, etc.
R3. Which, if any, of the current measurement approaches being used have made it possible to improve general education (curricula, specific courses and teaching strategies)?	S4. Which core student learning outcome measurement instruments and data collection methods have yielded the type of data that has made it possible to make improvements in your general education program, including curricula changes, specific course revisions, teaching strategies, etc.?
R5. What differences, if any, exist in the usefulness of instruments and methods of data collection based on the type (four-year and graduate level) and size of the institution?	S5. Describe improvements that have been made at your institutions as a result of data collected from core student learning outcomes assessment. For example, revised course content, revised curriculum, different delivery of instruction, etc. S6. As you assess your General Education Program and analyze the results, have you learned that there are some positive things that you are doing that are effective in the program? If yes, briefly describe those positive strategies.

Setting

This study was conducted during Fall Semester 2003 and Spring Semester 2004. The
population involved in this study was 62 institutions of higher learning that are members of the
Coalition of Urban and Metropolitan Universities (Appendix A). These institutions offer
undergraduate and graduate degrees and range in size from enrollments of approximately 750 to
41,000 students. The colleges and universities involved in this study are located in the following
28 states within the continental United States: Alaska, Arkansas, California, Colorado,
Connecticut, Florida, Georgia, Illinois, Indiana, Iowa, Kentucky, Louisiana, Maine, Maryland,
Massachusetts, Michigan, Missouri, Nebraska, Nevada, New York, North Carolina, Ohio,
Oregon, Rhode Island, South Carolina, Tennessee, Texas, and Washington.

Population of the Study

The metropolitan and urban colleges and universities targeted in this study all shared a
mission that is uniquely different from institutions that are not operating in the context of a
metropolis. These institutions strive to be responsive to the needs of the community and to adapt
their curriculum and instruction methodology to the diverse needs of metropolitan students. A
key underlying principle of the mission of metropolitan universities is to establish intimate ties
with elementary and secondary schools in an effort to improve the overall quality of education
(CUMU Website, n.d.). According to the CUMU website, "these institutions are located in or
near the urban center of a metropolitan statistical area (MSA) with a population of at least
250,000."

Metropolitan universities blend research-based learning with practical application,
synergizing interdisciplinary partnerships and forming alliances with outside public and private

64

organizations. This approach is effective in providing solutions to complex metropolitan problems. A primary priority of these institutions is to train and educate students to grow into informed, engaged citizens who become strong contributors to the betterment of society (CUMU Website, n.d.).

These institutions are public and private, with missions that include teaching, research, and professional service. Their primary goal is to serve students who are looking to complete their undergraduate and graduate education in the liberal arts and professional fields. The professional programs are impressively practice oriented and make broad use of clinical sites in the surrounding community. The population of students who attend these institutions is extremely diverse in age, ethnic and racial identity, and socioeconomic background and is highly representative of the demographic characteristics of the institutions' respective regions (CUMU Website, n.d.).

In an effort to enhance the response rate, contact was made with the individual who had a primary responsibility for assessment of the general education program. In each case, this person served in an administrative position (see Table 4).

Table 4

Administrative Positions of Respondents

Position	Frequency
Coordinator, General Education	1
Associate Dean	1
Director, Academic Affairs	1
Dean, Arts & Sciences	2
Senior Assoc. Vice Chancellor	1
Director, General Education	1
Director of Office for Integrating Learning	1
Undergraduate Dean	1
Director of Assessment	3
Associate Provost	4
Chair, Core Curriculum	1
Provost, Academic Affairs	1
Associate Dean, General Education	1
Director, Planning & Evaluation & Institutional Research	1
Associate Provost, Undergraduate Education	1
Assistant Dean, Arts & Sciences	1
Associate Vice President, Academic Affairs	1
Director, Undergraduate Assessment & Program Review	1

Data Collection

Telephone Calls to Establish Appropriate Contact and Agreement to Participate in Study

Dilman (2000) noted that contacting an organization to determine the appropriate

individual to receive the survey is very important. Dilman also described a study that involved

sending surveys to individuals at 238 universities who were not identified by name or by position

in advance. In order to address this challenge, a letter was sent to the president of the institution

prior to sending the survey requesting that the president identify the appropriate person and

forward the questionnaire to that person. Using both mail and telephone as follow-up resulted in

a response rate of 74%.

The researcher initiated phone calls to the institutions in order to identify the individuals who had a primary responsibility for the overall assessment of the core curriculum or general education program. Phone numbers for the institution were obtained by visiting each institution's website. The researcher contacted each institution and asked for the academic affairs department, the provost's office, or the chancellor's office. After contact was made with these offices, an explanation was provided regarding the purpose of the call. The researcher proceeded to ask for the name of the person who had a primary responsibility for directing the assessment effort for the general education program. The offices that were usually a good source of useful contact information were the assessment office or the general education area on the respective campuses. Each institution was receptive and provided enough information, including a phone number and in some instances an electronic-mail address, for the responsible individual.

Dilman (2000) asserted that using different methods of communication with potential respondents increases the response rate. Dilman further stated that when a researcher uses different approaches to communicate to potential respondents, an enhanced opportunity for communicating new information is the result.

Each individual who was identified as the general education program representative was contacted by phone or via an electronic message and asked to participate in the study. Contact was made with the potential participants who agreed to participate and provided detailed information (direct phone number, mailing address, and electronic-mail address).

Initial Mailing, Electronic Messages, and Follow-Up Contact

The researcher developed the initial mailing list from the detailed information gathered by telephone and electronic mail. The researcher completed an initial mailing of a cover letter, questionnaire, and addressed, stamped return envelope to 41 institutions. Thirteen institutions received only an electronic-mail message with an identical background for the research and a request for the college's participation in the study. The researcher was unsuccessful in making direct contact with the appropriate individuals at five institutions (University of Rhode Island; State University of New Jersey, Rutgers-Newark; University of New Orleans; University of South Florida, St. Petersburg; and William Paterson University). Three of the institutions (University of Washington, Tacoma; Washington State University, Spokane; and Washington State University, Vancouver) indicated that they were not involved in offering a general education curriculum because their focus was on upper-level programs (junior and senior year); therefore they did not receive a questionnaire. In an effort to maximize participation in the study, the researcher remained in close contact with potential respondents via follow-up electronic messages (Appendixes C, D, and E). The purpose of the study was restated and the URL for the study's questionnaire was provided.

In the initial stages of the organization of the research, all the potential respondents agreed to engage in additional interviews via telephone contact if deemed necessary by the researcher. If there was a need to obtain additional data and ask follow-up questions, the researcher made contact. Twenty-seven respondents out of the 54 institutions (50%) returned a completed survey. The researcher was able to use all of the responses.

Respondents were given the option to complete the survey either in the hard-copy format or the web-based version. The URL for the web-based questionnaire was http://oeas.ucf.edu/angela_doc.htm

Upon submission of the questionnaires via the website, the researcher created Microsoft Word documents from the database responses for each institution. The electronic mail responses

68

were already in a Microsoft Word document format. The hard copies that were received via mail were also converted to Microsoft Word documents. The documents were labeled with numbers to preserve the anonymity of the respondents. In addition to data that were collected in the form of the survey and hard-copy literature, additional information regarding the general education programs was collected from the respective websites. Demographics, including size of institution and level of degrees (undergraduate and graduate) offered, were collected from the respective websites.

The researcher loaded the Word documents into the *ATLAS.ti Version 5.0* software and began open coding the documents. The software automatically created a reference number as the data were coded.

Data Analysis

The researcher read the surveys several times to become familiar with the data. The data were analyzed using *ATLAS.ti Version 5.0*. This software was designed to analyze narrative and text data.

In order to label the data, a list of codes was developed and new codes emerged during the analysis (see Appendix G). Memos were created, using scrupulous record-keeping, documenting dates and noting the subcategories to which memos pertained. The researcher developed a list of potential comparison points during the process of reading transcripts (narrative data) from each institution.

To address issues of validity and trustworthiness, the researcher collected data from the self-reported survey responses, literature that was mailed with the survey and the institutions' general education program website. Prior to sending out the surveys, the researcher contacted each respondent and asked that they participate in this study. The respondents indicated their interest in the study and stated that they would provide answers to the best of their ability.

Individuals who were integrally involved in assessment of the core curriculum gave the responses that were provided. The respondents served in high level administrative positions, which required a level of expertise in the area of evaluation and assessment (see Table 4).

The methods of data collection included a web-based survey that when submitted was imported into a database for easy retrieval. The web-based submissions were automatically dated upon submission. The completed surveys that were returned via electronic mail were dated upon accessing them. The hard-copy surveys were dated upon arrival and scanned. All of the responses were imported into the software (*ATLAS.ti Version 5.0*), which was used by the researcher to analyze the data. The data retrieved from the institutions' websites and the hard-copy literature were scanned and imported into the analysis software.

During the analysis phase, the researcher was mentored by an assistant professor from the University of Central Florida. The mentor served as a teacher of the grounded theory model and as a systematic critic, persisting with questions regarding the analyses and ensuring that the researcher did not lean toward personal biases and the literature. Borman, LeCompte and Goetze (1986) stressed the importance of using mentors, seeking external criticism of the emerging analysis, and achieving separation from the data. The researcher attempted to, as much as possible within the constraints of time available, to detach from the data in order to maintain an objective perspective during the analysis phase.

Borman et al. (1986) asserted that translatability and comparability is as important to qualitative research as validity or generalizability is for researchers from other paradigms. They stated that translatability

70

requires that methods, categories and characteristics of phenomena and groups be identified so explicitly that comparisons can be made across groups and disciplines with confidence. Comparability requires that standard and nonidiosyncratic terminology be used wherever possible and that the boundaries and characteristics of what is studied be crystal clear. (p. 48)

In Chapter 4 the findings of the analysis are presented in the form of tables and figures

and supported by narrative description. In Chapter 5 analyzed results of the data were used as the

basis for conclusions. The conclusions will serve as underpinnings for future research.

CHAPTER 4

DATA PRESENTATION AND ANALYSIS

Introduction

This chapter presents the results of an open-ended survey of administrators at 27 institutions of higher education. These institutions were all members of the Coalition of Metropolitan and Urban Universities (CUMU). The purpose of the study was to determine (a) what instruments and methods of data collection are being used to assess core general education student-learning outcomes at urban and metropolitan universities and (b) the extent to which these approaches to measurement are producing data that can be used for improvement purposes.

Chapter 4 is divided into three sections: the responses to the research questions, findings of the analysis, and summary of the findings.

Findings of the Research Questions

The results of the research questions were derived from analyzing responses to the six questions included in the research instrument. Some survey questions (S2, S3, S4, S5, and S6) related directly to the research questions (S2 with R1 and R4; S3 with R2 and S4; S5 and S6 with R3 and R5). The remaining survey question (S1) was used to obtain more in-depth information about each institution.

As described in Chapter 3, the author used grounded theory for data analysis. Since this approach allows theories to emerge rather than predicting a theory, the findings presented here

72

first answer the research proposal questions and then lead to the presentation of the theory, which was developed using grounded theory.

Findings of the Research Questions With Related Survey Questions

This section presents the results for each of the research questions.

Findings of Research Question 1 and 4 With Related Survey Question 2

Research Question R1: What core general education student-learning outcomes are being assessed at urban and metropolitan colleges and universities?

Research Question R4: What differences, if any, exist in the institutions' stated intended core student-learning outcomes based on the type (four-year and graduate level) and size of the institution?

Related Survey Question S2: What core general education student-learning outcomes have been developed and are being measured at your institution? For example, the ability to think critically, the ability to communicate effectively both written and verbal, the ability to solve quantitative problems, etc.

Both cognitive and affective learning outcomes were identified as important to the institutions (see Table 5). The researcher categorized these survey responses using Bloom's taxonomy. The outcomes that were related to acquired knowledge included art appreciation; behavior science; communication (oral and written); critical thinking; cultural awareness; economics; environmental awareness; foreign language; general knowledge of political, economic, social, and geographical facts and issues; history; humanities; modes of learning; psychology; quantitative/mathematics; reading; science; and social and domestic issues. The top four most frequently cited outcomes were 1) communications (oral and written), 2) critical thinking, and 3) quantitative skills and life-long learner (equal frequency). Table 5 provides the frequencies for each outcome cited.

Table 5

Intended Student-Learning Outcomes Categorized Under Knowledge, Skills, Behavior, and

Beliefs and Values (Population = 54, n = 27)

Purpose	Core student-learning outcomes	Frequency
Knowledge		
	communication (oral and written)	23
	critical thinking	20
	quantitative/math	12
	cultural awareness	10
	art appreciation	9
	humanities	7
	science	9
	reading	7
	history	5
	foreign language	4
	behavior science	4
	environmental appreciation	3
	social and domestic issues	2
	American institution	1
Skills		
	communication (oral and written)	23
	critical thinking	20
	analytical	11
	problem solving	6
	technology	5
	tools for knowledge	4
	reasoning	4
	independent thinker	3
	leadership	3
	creative inquiry	2
	interrelate physical, mental, emotional, and quality of life	2
	interpret quantitative and qualitative data	2
	interrelate science, technology, and society	1
	listening	1
	synthesis of information	1
Behavior		
	personal development	6
	collaborate with others	4
	decision making	2
	community service	2

Purpose	Core student-learning outcomes	Frequency
Beliefs and values (affective)		
	life-long learner	12
	global appreciation	11
	diversity awareness	10
	ethics and values	7
	leadership	3
	community service	2
	self learner	2
	fitness for life	1

The top three most frequently cited intended learning outcomes under the knowledge category were 1) communication (written and verbal), 2) quantitative and mathematics, and 3) critical thinking. The top three most frequently cited intended learning outcomes under the skills category were 1) communications, 2) critical thinking, and 3) analytical.

The top two most frequently cited intended learning outcomes under the behavior category were 1) personal development and 2) the ability to collaborate with others.

The top three most frequently cited intended outcome under beliefs and values were 1) life-long learner, 2) global awareness, and 3) diversity appreciation.

All the institutions offered undergraduate and graduate level degrees. The researcher did not observe any distinction between the learning outcomes based on the size of the institution.

Findings of Research Question 2 with Related Survey Question 3

Research Question R2: What instruments and methods of data collection are being used to assess core general education student-learning outcomes at urban and metropolitan universities?

Related Survey Question S3: What types of measurement approaches (instruments, data collection methods) are being used to assess these core student-learning outcomes at your institution? For example, portfolios, standardized tests, essays, embedded test questions, etc.

The measurement approaches that were reported by the institutions were in two categories—direct approaches to measurement and indirect approaches. These categories emerged based on the types of assessment of student-learning outcomes. The direct measurement approaches included tests and exams (both local and standardized), licensure and certification exams, embedded questions and portfolios. One institution reported that it used both hard copy and electronic versions of portfolios as well as program- and institutional-level portfolios. Other direct approaches to assessment included course-based assessments, essays, direct observations, classroom assessments, research papers, internships and service learning, grade-point averages, senior assignments, and capstone classes. The indirect measurement approaches were surveys (both local and national), transcript analysis, case studies, focus groups, interviews, syllabi analysis, completion and retention rates, and student activity and study logs. Table 6 presents the measurement approaches with the frequency of reported uses of the instruments or methodologies. The 27 institutions that responded to the survey offered undergraduate and graduate degrees. The researcher observed that there were direct approaches (actual measurement of the knowledge and skills required) and indirect approaches (students' perceptions about their knowledge and skill attainment, alumni perceptions, employer and parents' perceptions). Some of these measurement approaches are considered traditional (standardized tests) and some are considered non-traditional. (See Chapter 2: Methods of Assessment.) The researcher did not observe any distinction between the measurement approaches based on the size of the institution.

Table 6

Approaches Used to Measure Intended Student-Learning Outcomes Reported by 19 Institutions

(Population = 54, n = 27)

Assessment approaches	Methods/Instruments	Frequency
Direct approaches		
Tests		
	[a]Standardized tests	17
	Locally developed tests	9
	State mandated tests	3
	Pre/Post	2
	Certification and licensure exams	1
Other Direct Approaches		
	[a]Essay	10
	[a]Portfolios	9
	Embedded questions	4
	[a]Course-based assessment	2
	GPA	2
	Research paper	1
	[a]Senior assignments	2
	Capstone	1
	Grade distributions	1
	Classroom assessment	1
	Direct observation	1
	Internships & service learning	1
Indirect approaches		
[a]Surveys		
	Local surveys (faculty, alumni)	10
	National survey of student engagement (NSSE)	4
	Graduating senior survey	3
	Student satisfaction survey	2
Other indirect approaches		
	Case study	1
	Focus group	1
	Interview	1
	Retention rate	1
	Completion rate	1
	Student activity and study log	1
	Syllabi analysis	1
	Transcript analysis	1

[a] Reported by the respondent as yielding meaningful data

Findings of Research Question 3 and 5 with Related Survey Questions 4, 5, and 6

R3. Which, if any, of the current measurement approaches being used have made it possible to improve general education (curricula, specific courses and teaching strategies)?

R5. What differences, if any, exist in the usefulness of instruments and methods of data collection based on the type (four-year and graduate level) and size of the institution?

S4. Which core student learning outcome measurement instruments and data collection methods have yielded the type of data that has made it possible to make improvements in your general education program, including curricula changes, specific course revisions, teaching strategies, etc.?

S5. Describe improvements that have been made at your institutions as a result of data collected from core student learning outcomes assessment. For example, revised course content, revised curriculum, different delivery of instruction, etc.

S6. As you assess your General Education Program and analyze the results, have you learned that there are some positive things that you are doing that are effective in the program? If yes, briefly describe those positive strategies.

It was reported by three institutions (Aqua University, Amber University, and Purple University [for the sake of anonymity, pseudonyms were used for institutions' formal names]) that all of the assessment was meaningful because the data that were collected resulted in change that was considered to be a positive change. However specific reference was made to the following methods of assessment that were meaningful: 1) Measurement of Intellectual Development (standardized test), 2) surveys, 3) essays, 4) portfolios, 5) course-based assessment, 6) grade distribution, 7) the analytic writing instrument, and 8) senior assignment. One of the respondents reported that the portfolios that were referred to were being used on both a program and an institutional level in both hard-copy and electronic formats. See Table 7 for respondents' reporting of measurement approaches that led to change. These assessment methods were used to collect data for intended-learning outcomes, and the data indicated that there were specific gaps or weaknesses either in the pedagogy, the curriculum, or the assessment process.

Table 7

Changes Reported to Have Been Implemented as the Result of Conducting Assessment

(Population = 54, n=27)

Reported changes	Number of institutions
Increased faculty involvement	13
Revised curriculum	7
Revised course	6
Revised pedagogy	5
Began interdisciplinary initiative	4
Created assessment task force	3
Reexamined program	3
Increased awareness of learning outcomes	3
Added new writing and math center	3
Enhanced faculty workshops with focus on assessment	3
Revised approach to assessment	2
Offered assessment retreat & workshops	2
Added new measurement approaches	2
Changed textbook	1
Added ESL class	1
Improved technology	1
Changed level of course	1
Scholarship of assessment	1
Conducted reevaluation of course	1
Changed process for freshmen registration	1
Integrated student and institutional portfolios	1
Realized value of assessment	1

The respondents reported the following changes that were made as a result of conducting assessment (reported changes are listed by the order of frequency from the greatest to the least cited): increased faculty involvement; revised curriculum; revised courses; revised pedagogy; initiation of interdisciplinary approach to assessment; created assessment task force; reexamined program; increased awareness of learning outcomes and added a new writing and math center.

Whenever the respondent cited a specific type of change that was implemented as a result of collected data, it is included in Table 7.

Other changes included an enhancement of faculty workshops with focus on assessment; revised approach to assessment; assessment retreat and workshops and added new measurement approaches. Additional changes included changed textbook; added ESL class; improved technology; changed level of course; stressed the importance of the scholarship of assessment; conducted reevaluation of course; changed process for freshmen registration; integrated student and institutional portfolios; and realized the value of assessment.

The 16 institutions that reported changes offered undergraduate and graduate level degrees. The researcher did not observe any distinction between the usefulness of instruments and methods of data collection based on the size of the institution.

Twenty-three (85%) of the 27 respondents reported that to some extent they assessed core learning outcomes of the general education program (see Table 8). Nineteen (83%) of the 23 institutions reported that they had a process in place to routinely assess student learning and used either direct approaches, indirect assessment approaches, or both. Sixteen (70%) of the 23 institutions reported changes. Three (13%) of the 23 institutions that were conducting some type of assessment did not report changes for various reasons. One of the three institutions could not report on improvement, as the assessment was course based and they could not track any changes. One of the three institutions reported that 70% of its incoming students were transfer students and had enrolled at the institutions after having completed all of the core curriculum requirements. This institution stated that the data that were collected provided an overview of how students were doing; however, it could not be used to make changes. One of the three institutions collected assessment data in areas of mathematics and English composition using only a standardized test.

Table 8

Stages of Assessment Based on the 27 Institutions' Level of Engagement in Formal Assessment Along With the Types of Measurement Approaches Used in Stages One, Two and Three (Population = 54, n = 27)

Stage of assessment based on the 27 institutions engagement in formal assessment	Number of institutions in this stage and using this assessment approach(es)	Measurement approaches used to assess intended learning outcomes	Were there any changes made as a result of conducting assessment?
Stage One	13	direct and indirect	yes
(assessing, making data-driven changes)	3	direct	yes
Stage Two	1	direct and indirect	no
(assessing, no changes implemented)	2	direct	no
Stage Three (early stage, not enough time to determine if changes are needed)	4	direct and indirect	no
Stage Four (planning stage)	3	none	no
Stage Five (no assessment process)	1	none	no

Eleven institutions (41%) of the 27 that responded did not report data-driven changes. Four of the institutions reported that they were in the early stages of assessment and that it was too soon to tell if the process was effective. Three of the institutions were in the planning stages of assessment and planned to begin conducting assessment by Fall 2004 or in the near future.

One institution had no assessment structure for assessment at this time. Table 8 shows the status of the implementation of assessment among the 27 institutions.

The respondents described the positive activities that were effective in the general education program (see Table 9). These included the realization that outcomes are not well defined, using diagnostic testing, taking annual steps in goal achievement, using baseline measures, offering assessment retreats, and holding workshops. Others included practicing an active, learning-centered philosophy; establishing new writing and mathematics centers; implementing a task force on assessment; and fostering a scholarship of assessment. Additional positive activities included mentoring, involving those who were hesitant to participate in the assessment process, reporting results of assessment publicly, increasing faculty involvement, and realizing that assessment is valuable. The positive activity of "public reporting" is important as it apprises stakeholders of what is going on within the institution regarding assessment and the attention that leadership devotes to continuous improvement.

Table 9

Positive Activities That Were Reported by Nine Institutions as the Result of Conducting

Assessment (Population = 54, n = 27)

Category	Reported activities	Number of institutions
Assessment process		
	creation of task force on assessment	5
	assessment workshops	5
	realization that outcomes are not well defined	3
	scholarship of assessment	2
	assessment retreat	2
	diagnostic testing	1
	annual steps in goal achievement	1
	baseline measures	1
Teaching		
	writing and math centers	2
	active learning center	1
Culture		
	increased faculty involvement	5
	realization that assessment is valuable	3
	involving doubters in the process	1
	public reporting	1

Following is the presentation of the theory that emerged using grounded theory.

Introduction to the Grounded Theory

Twenty-three (85%) of the 27 institutions of higher learning participating in this study

reported that they assessed the general education program curriculum. The remaining 4 (15%)

reported that they were not assessing the core curriculum. They were not assessing for different

reasons. Sixteen schools out of the 23 institutions indicated that they had implemented changes that were guided by assessment findings. The remaining seven did not report changes for various reasons (see Table 8).

Having the capability to make changes in an effort to improve pedagogical practices, institutions found the core curriculum and assessment to be important because they believed that this process would enhance their capacity to do a better job in the area of teaching and learning, thereby addressing society's concerns regarding the preparation of students for efficacy in the workplace and students' general success in society.

Furthermore, if the Coalition of Urban and Metropolitan Universities (CUMU) were aware of the stage that its member institutions are in (stages one through five), then the leadership would be in a better position to appropriate funding, provide training, develop assessment partnerships for the purpose of learning how to improve the assessment process, and report publicly to the primary stakeholders. The institutions would also be better prepared to address assessment issues relative to accreditation requirements.

Stages of Implementation of Assessment of General Education

In this study the researcher developed a central category focused on "stages of implementation of assessment of the general education program." There were five stages:

1. Institutions that were conducting assessment and were able to implement changes that were based on the findings of assessment

2. Institutions that were conducting assessment but which, because of current conditions, could not make changes based on collected data

3. Institutions that had just begun to engage in assessing the core curriculum but had not had enough time to evaluate the effectiveness of the process

84

4. Institutions that were still in the planning phase of implementing assessment activity

5. Institutions that did not have an assessment process in place and had no immediate plans to implement one

Below are the responses of the institutions under the stage that they indicated. The responses from the institutions, which were analyzed using the *ATLAS.ti Version 5.0* software, were referenced using the numbers that were assigned by the software to the quotations (e.g., 4P2:4). Additionally, in order to preserve anonymity, pseudonyms (colors) were used for institutions' formal names.

Institutions Assessing the Core Curriculum That Have Made Changes

Based on Collected Data (Stage One)

<u>Sage University:</u> Our general education program is designed to promote, enhance and assess student learning in a common set of ways of knowing and intellectual skills that are the foundation of and transcend specific disciplines and professions. We focus on improvement and achievement in these common learning outcomes throughout the undergraduate curriculum. (4:P7:7:2) Each department/academic program delineates changes in pedagogy and curricula as a result of assessment of our PULS [principles of undergraduate learning]. They range from changing the textbook to instituting PBL [project-based learning]. (4P7:12)

<u>Teal University:</u> While the student who earns a baccalaureate degree at Teal will have examined the specialized field of a major and pursued some elective studies of interest, the faculty believes that the pursuit of a degree would be incomplete without study of a common body of knowledge which supports our humanity. Teal provides for every student regardless of field of study the opportunity to build a foundation, which constitutes that common body of experience. (4P8:8:1)…Modifications have been made in Mathematics 121 which is Algebra to create a second course Mathematics 121S which is Precalculus Algebra. Revisions to the English courses are being considered. Additionally, the Provost is in the process of creating a General Education Committee to reexamine General Education. (4P8:3) In both English and Mathematics labs have been created with highly qualified tutors to assist students. Computers have been installed with supportive software that correlates to our coursework. (4P:8:2)

<u>Black University:</u> The reports from the two previous assessment exercises identified a number of problems with the design of the assessment plan and with the nature of the

samples collected for assessment.... The assessment group believes that the first step toward an effective outcomes assessment strategy for the general education curriculum is a process that will foster discovery of the range of current understandings of the curriculum and pedagogical practices within the general education curriculum. (4P3:5)

Violet University: It seems that we have arrived at a meaningful assessment program that indicates we are having a significant and positive impact on our students in terms of our goals and objectives. The challenge, however, is to do better. Our immediate plans are to continue the assessment process, but also to institute a system of regular department meetings in which the results of the process can be discussed along with ideas as to how they might be improved. While this will be an imprecise process, we believe that the dissemination of accurate and regular evidence combined with discussion and reflection by both full-time and part-time faculty will create circumstances under which already-effective classroom teaching will be further improved. (4P4:4:1)

Aqua University: More emphasis has been placed on Learning Communities which link classes in a thematic fashion. This allows students to see the connections in knowledge and to develop a group of campus friends. Some multi-section classes have more aggressively monitored the sections for conformity to one another. There is a much more focused awareness of the importance and objectives of General Education. (4:P17:4) It is of key importance that as many faculty as possible are involved in the assessment and evaluation process. (4:P17:3)

Ivory University: We are in the process of revising our general education curriculum and are using our assessment data to guide change. We will be focusing more on critical thinking, reasoning, and writing skills and will be strongly recommending specific teaching strategies to foster this growth. (4P30:2)

Gold University: We are in the middle of a complete rewrite of assessment of the GEP. This was triggered in part by the realization that good assessment was possible (composition the notable example) and the additional realization that most areas of the GEP are not assessed well. Attempts to assess showed us that our GEP learning objectives are not well enough defined, which is something of a success—at least, the first steps towards success. (4P22:13)

Gray University: One recommendation is the immediate implementation of a degree audit system that will provide systematic data on the courses students complete prior to their admission to Gray University (4P24:1). Another recommendation was the implementation of baseline measurements for student competencies in reading, writing, and mathematics so that exit measures of learning outcomes in these skills can be meaningfully analyzed and used to make curricular changes. (4P24:2) The current analysis of existing assessment procedures has led the GELS Committee and the Assessment Committee to jointly sponsor an all day university retreat on improving the assessment of general education outcomes. The retreat was held in November and an Ad Hoc Work Group is developing plans to implement new testing and analysis procedures. (4P24:8)

Beige University: We currently have a Baccalaureate Objectives task force that is examining faculty concerns as informed by assessment results. It is unlikely that the general education program will undergo major transformation at this time. This is partly due to findings that it is not so much the structure of the program but, rather, its execution that can be improved to produce significant gains in student learning. In addition, we sponsored three Faculty Assessment Scholars who investigated, as scholars, the question, "To what extent and by what means do students learn to improve their writing at Beige University?" These investigations not only provided data regarding one important aspect of general education but also resulted in three peer-reviewed publications, thus reinforcing the Scholarhip [sic] of Teaching theme on our campus. (4P28:1)

Tan University: Concerned that students could number-crunch but did not know WHY particular statistical methods were applicable in certain situations but not in others. Revised curriculum to include more statistical thinking in Research Methods class. Focused subsequent assessment efforts through the Senior Assignment on statistical thinking. After two years, improvements met level of faculty expectation and focus shifted to another aspect of the curriculum. Music: Jazz focus requires what other departments would call 'teamwork' because jazz scoring and performing differs from orchestral scoring and performing. Music department was producing fine virtuoso performers but did not seem to produce students with necessary 'teamwork' skills for jazz performances. Based on assessment findings, department shifted curriculum to include more ensemble requirements. This resulted in more teamwork. (4P28:2)

Blue University: In the past, assessment led to changes in class size; changes to the curriculum with the addition of new GE courses; and, most dramatically, the introduction of the new GE Program. (4P36:1)

Institutions Assessing the Core Curriculum That Had No Changes (Stage Two)

Fuchsia University: No changes have been made. Fuchsia University is a large institution with over 20,000 students. Approximately 70% of its graduates transferred to the college having completed portions of a general education program elsewhere. The data provide an overview of how well our graduates are prepared, but are not specific enough to indicate that a certain specific course or set of courses needs improvement.

Maroon University: It is difficult for me to answer this question since the assessment activities are carried on at the course level. One of the reasons for the first component of the assessment portfolio, however, is to give the department the opportunity to describe the changes they have made in the class and why. Hopefully, these revisions are made in response to their assessment results. My response to item 4 also applies here. I am confident that some departments have revised their core content. Several classes in the program have been dropped – although usually for a combination of reasons including poor enrollment, staff problems, etc.

<u>Yellow University:</u> We have used the CBASE exam for about 15 years. The state's Performance Funding program requires each institution to test all graduating seniors with this or one of several other instruments. Results are reported to the higher education commission then compared to national norms for evaluation and assignment of points. Points are converted to dollars in the next FY appropriation. We really have not been able to effectively use the test results to accomplish this end. (4P:31:1)

<u>White University:</u> So far we have only collected systematically outcomes assessment data in areas of mathematics and English composition based on entry level placement exams. This is what we are planning to do as we move forward in an organized systematic fashion for the entire GE program. To be determined.

Institutions in the Early Stages of Assessment of the Core Curriculum

That Had No Changes Based on Assessment Findings (Stage Three)

<u>Pink University:</u> This is basically new to us so we have no results yet.

<u>Silver University:</u> We are in the process of developing a formal assessment process for distribution courses in conjunction with our NCA review.

Institutions Planning to Implement Assessment of the Core Curriculum

With No Changes Based on Assessment Findings (Stage Four)

<u>Red University:</u> The assessment program is still under development. In addition to student survey results and special assessments, it will include two components: 1) category-based assessments developed by each GEC category committee... and 2) surveys of departments that indicate achievement levels of graduating seniors as assessed for the learning goals in 2.

<u>Jade University:</u> The General Education Council has just developed and approved the General Education Goals and Outcomes during fall semester, 2003. Assessment methods for these outcomes have not yet been determined, but that is the next step in our assessment process. It is expected that assessment methods will be determined and carried out during spring and fall semesters, 2004.

Institution That Had Not Developed an Assessment Process (Stage Five)

Taupe University: The plan is to focus on General Education assessment in the future. The institution has been investing more time in developing uniform department-based outcomes assessment plans.

Stages of Implementation of Assessment of the Core Curriculum

at 27 Metropolitan and Urban Universities

If one were to describe the stages of assessment of the core curriculum among the 27 metropolitan and urban universities, there would be five. In stage one institutions were actively engaged in assessing student-learning outcomes and have been successful in identifying weaknesses and made changes in the pedagogy, curriculum, and assessment processes (Gray, Black, Gold, Ivory, Aqua, Violet, and Teal Universities). This capability is important because the institutions were in a better position to address the needs of the society regarding student preparedness for the workplace and the society at large.

Survey question one (S1) posed a question regarding the purpose of the general education program, and all of the institutions stated that the purpose of the core curriculum was 1) to impart certain knowledge, 2) to develop certain skills, 3) to affect certain behavior, and 4) to affect certain beliefs and values (see Table 3).

The second stage included institutions that were involved in assessment (Fuchsia, Maroon, Yellow, and White Universities) but that had not made any changes that were driven by assessment data. These institutions were 1) using a placement exam, 2) conducting course-based assessment that could not be tracked, 3) assessing students broadly and thus were unable to use the findings effectively, and 4) measuring learning outcomes with one direct method of assessment (the CBASE).

Institutions in the third stage were in the early stages of assessment and could not determine the efficacy of the process (Pink and Silver Universities). Institutions in the fourth stage were in the planning stages of assessment (Red and Jade Universities). They were 1) selecting measurement approaches and 2) finalizing implementation plans. Finally, in the fifth stage institutions were not involved in an assessment process at all (Taupe University). This institution reported that it had plans to develop an assessment process in the near future.

Summary of Findings

Twenty-three (85%) of the 27 institutions that participated in this study reported that they conducted assessment of the core curriculum. They focused on assessing student outcomes related to specific knowledge, skills, behaviors, and beliefs and values. In an effort to find out what problems existed in the institutions' general education program, direct and indirect measurement approaches were used to assess learning outcomes. Sixteen institutions reported changes in 1) pedagogical practices, 2) the curriculum, or 3) the assessment process. In some instances they reported that they were able to make assessment-related changes not only in one of these areas, but in two or all three areas. Three institutions were assessing but had not implemented any data-drive changes due to specific reasons cited in Table 8.

Four additional institutions reported they had not made any data-drive changes. These four were at three distinctly different stages 1) early stages, 2) planning stages, and 3) no assessment process was established.

Conclusions, discussion, implications, and recommendations for future research are discussed in Chapter 5.

CHAPTER 5

CONCLUSIONS AND RECOMMENDATIONS

This chapter presents a summary of the study, conclusions, and a discussion of those findings. The chapter concludes with recommendations for future research.

Summary of the Study

This qualitative study was conducted during the Fall Semester 2003 and the Spring Semester 2004. The population involved 62 institutions of higher learning that are members of the Coalition of Urban and Metropolitan Universities (Appendix A). The researcher was unsuccessful in making direct contact with the appropriate individuals at five institutions (University of Rhode Island; State University of New Jersey, Rutgers-Newark; University of New Orleans; University of South Florida, St. Petersburg; and William Paterson University). Three institutions (University of Washington, Tacoma; Washington State University, Spokane; and Washington State University, Vancouver) indicated that they were not involved in offering a general education curriculum because their focus was on upper-level programs (junior and senior year); therefore they did not receive a questionnaire.

A survey instrument was sent by the researcher to 54 institutions via U.S. mail and electronic mail. Responders submitted their answers to the questions contained in the survey via a hard-copy version and a web-based version. Twenty-seven institutions sent their completed surveys back to the researcher either as hard-copy documents or web-based documents. These responses were analyzed and served as the basis of the conclusions included in this chapter.

The purpose of the study was to determine (a) what instruments and methods of data collection were being used to assess core general education student-learning outcomes at urban and metropolitan universities and (b) the extent to which these approaches to measurement were producing data that can be used for improvement purposes. The researcher sought to answer five research questions:

1. What core general education student-learning outcomes are being assessed at urban and metropolitan colleges and universities?

2. What instruments and methods of data collection are being used to assess core general education student-learning outcomes at urban and metropolitan colleges and universities?

3. Which, if any, of the current measurement approaches being used have made it possible to improve general education (curricula, specific courses, and teaching strategies)?

4. What differences, if any, exist in the institutions' stated intended core student-learning outcomes based on the type (four-year and graduate level) and size of the institution?

5. What differences, if any, exist in the usefulness of instruments and methods of data collection based on the type (four-year and graduate level) and size of the institution?

A survey, which was designed by the researcher based on a review of the literature, was used to guide this study. The following questions were included in the survey:

1. Briefly provide a description of the purpose of your general education program.

2. What core general education student-learning outcomes have been developed and are being measured at your institution? For example, the ability to think critically, the ability

to communicate effectively both written and verbal, the ability to solve quantitative problems, etc.

3. What types of measurement approaches (instruments, data-collection methods) are being used to assess these core student-learning outcomes at your institution? For example, portfolios, standardized tests, essays, and embedded test questions.

4. Which core student-learning outcome measurement instruments and data-collection methods have yielded the type of data that has made it possible to make changes in your general education program, including curriculum changes, specific course revisions, teaching strategies?

5. Describe improvements that have been made at your institution as a result of data collected from core student-learning outcomes assessment. For example, revised course content, revised curriculum and different delivery of instruction.

6. As you assess your General Education Program and analyze the results, have you learned that there are some positive things that you are doing that are effective in the program? If yes, briefly describe those positive strategies.

Conclusions of the Study from the Descriptive Analysis

The following conclusions are based on the data analysis that was presented in Chapter 4.

1. The purposes of general education programs were a) to impart knowledge, b) to develop skill, c) to affect behavior, and d) to affect beliefs and values to enhance the capacity of students to be successful in society.

2. Specific learning outcomes were identified as important to the fulfillment of the institutions' general education programs' purposes. The outcomes that were related to

acquired knowledge included art appreciation; behavior science; communication (oral and written); critical thinking; cultural awareness; economics; environmental awareness; foreign language; general political, economic, and history studies; humanities; quantitative/mathematics; reading; science; social and domestic issues. The student-learning outcomes associated with skills included analysis, communication (oral and written), creative inquiry, critical thinking, decision making, information gathering, interpretation of quantitative and qualitative data, listening, problem solving, reasoning, research, synthesis of information, technology, and tools for knowledge. The student-learning outcomes that were related to behavior included the ability of students to collaborate with others; provide community service; be fit for life; be an independent thinker; interrelate physical, mental, emotional, and quality of life issues; interrelate science, technology, and society; demonstrate leadership; and develop personally. The learning outcomes associated with beliefs and values included an awareness and appreciation of diversity, ethics, and values; global issues; life-long learning; and self-learning.

3. The measurement approaches that were reported by the institutions were in two distinct categories—direct approaches to measurement and indirect approaches. The direct measurement approaches included tests and exams (both local and standardized), licensure and certification exams, portfolios (both hard copy and electronic as well as program and institutional), course-based assessments, essays, direct observations, classroom assessments, research papers, internships and service learning, exams for licensure and certification, grade-point averages, senior assignments, and capstone classes. The indirect measurement approaches were surveys (both local and national),

transcript analysis, case studies, focus groups, interviews, syllabus analysis, completion and retention rates, and student activity and study logs.

4. The following measurement approaches were cited as methods of data collection that were meaningful: 1) senior assignments, 2) essays, 3) surveys, and 4) portfolios. The portfolios were implemented on both a program and an institutional level. The portfolios were in both hard-copy and electronic forms. See Table 6 for measurement approaches that were cited as meaningful.

5. The respondents reported that the following changes were made as a result of conducting assessment: revised curriculum, added courses, changed class size, adopted new textbook, improved technology, increased awareness of student-learning outcomes, changed level of course, and added writing and math centers. Other changes included offering an assessment retreat, creation of an assessment task force, an increase in faculty involvement, an increase in the interdisciplinary approach to assessment, a revision in the assessment process, new measurement approaches, a reevaluation of courses, a reexamination of the general education program, a revision of the curriculum, a revision of the pedagogy, an offering of assessment workshops, and a development of plans for revising the assessment process. Additional changes included increased faculty involvement, revised process for freshmen registration, and the implementation of an integrated student and institutional–level portfolio system.

6. The respondents described the positive activities that were effective in the general education program (see Table 9). These included the realization that outcomes are not well defined, the implementation of diagnostic testing, annual steps in goal achievement, the use of baseline measures, and the offering of assessment retreats and workshops.

Additionally, positive activities that were acknowledged by respondents included the practice of an active learning–centered philosophy, the establishment of new writing and mathematics centers, the implementation of a task force on assessment, and the fostering of a scholarship of assessment. Other reported positive activities included mentoring, involving those who were hesitant to participate in the assessment process, reporting results of assessment publicly, increasing faculty involvement, and realizing that assessment is valuable.

Conclusions of the Study From the Grounded Theory

There were five stages of implementation of assessment. These stages are indicated below:

Stage One: Institutions that were actively engaged in the assessment process and making changes guided by assessment findings.

Stage Two: Institutions that were conducting assessment but were not able to collect meaningful data that led to changes.

Stage Three: Institutions that were in the early stage of assessment and enough time had not elapsed to collect data that led to changes.

Stage Four: Institutions that were in the planning stages for implementation of the assessment process.

Stage Five: Institutions that had no assessment plan established but had intentions to start one in the near future.

<u>Discussion</u>

The discussion that follows centers around the findings of this study. The discussion is organized by two questions posed in the problem statement. The two research questions' foci were on the types of measurement approaches that were used among the 62 institutions that were members of the Coalition of Urban and Metropolitan Universities and the extent to which these measurement approaches were yielding data that lead to changes in the general education program. The discussion ends with the findings of the grounded theory analysis.

Measurement Approaches Used in Assessing General Education

Results of the study indicated that the 23 or 85% of the institutions that participated in the study used direct and indirect measurement approaches to measure core student-learning outcomes in the core curriculum. The general education curriculum was related directly to the purpose of the general education program. The purposes of the general education programs aligned with the outcomes that faculty and administrators held to be valuable for students matriculating at a metropolitan or urban university. Once the purpose was established, the focus was on student-learning outcomes that connected with those purposes.

Since students were expected to know, do, think, and feel a certain way upon completion of an undergraduate education, the institutions shared their philosophies regarding the need for the curricula to be closely aligned with the asserted purpose. The results of the survey indicated that the curricula were structured so that students were provided the experiences that would enhance knowledge, behavior, and values. The results of the analysis regarding intended student-learning outcomes strongly resembled what the literature stressed. It was clear that the 27 institutions that responded had well-established purposes and core student-learning outcomes

97

that extended from those purposes. The challenge that these institutions faced was how to measure the intended learning outcomes in their effort to identify weaknesses in the curriculum or deficiencies in pedagogical practices and strategies.

The measurement approaches, both direct and indirect, were used to measure cognitive and affective student-learning outcomes of the core curriculum. The review of the literature (see Chapter 2: Assessment that Leads to Improvement) supported the fact that general education programs are assessing core learning outcomes with various measurement approaches, including direct and indirect methods. The literature also pointed to the fact that institutions would be better served if they chose to identify appropriate methods that are non-traditional (e.g., standardized tests and student surveys). The literature noted the importance of institutions' assessing the effectiveness of the curriculum and pedagogical culture by seeking to find out, using indirect measurement approaches, perceptions of all of the key stakeholders (students, faculty, alumni, employers). The findings of this study were consistent with the literature. All institutions used both direct and indirect approaches and traditional and non-traditional methodologies.

Respondents articulated concerns regarding the overall lack of coordination and collaboration among faculty members in the identification of learning objectives. Additionally, respondents were concerned that, in many instances, faculty members were not in agreement with the measurement approaches that were being used and how they should be used.

Faculty input and consensus regarding the core curriculum and the assessment process was an important topic in the review of literature (Huba & Freed, 2000). According to the literature, faculty involvement served to ensure uniformity in the curriculum and the design of the assessment process, including rubrics, student samples, and criteria for assignments. A few

98

institutions cited course-by-course assessment of the core curriculum as the reason it was difficult to determine the meaningfulness of specific measurement approaches. It was evident that those who were integrally involved with assessing the general education curriculum felt that it was crucial to take an interdisciplinary approach. Faculty across departments needed to be engaged in the assessment process, and if they were not involved, it would be difficult to track the effectiveness of the assessment practices. The literature was clear on the topic of the power of faculty collaboration and how faculty should use assessment to direct their teaching strategies.

Many institutions used portfolios to assess the writing learning outcome. Results of the survey indicated that faculty members were engaged in a process of developing rubrics, disseminating and explaining learning objectives to students, and providing appropriate classroom experiences so that students could meet writing expectations prior to graduation. One institution noted that it had implemented both a program-level portfolio and an institutional-level portfolio and that it integrated the two for an enhanced assessment approach. Again, the literature stressed the importance of 1) faculty involvement, 2) the development of meaningful rubrics, and 3) the provision of classroom experiences that are aligned with intended learning outcomes.

Three institutions noted that they were directed to use specific traditional measurement approaches by the state of residence. This requirement dictated which learning outcomes would be assessed and the measurement approaches that were to be used. Standardized instruments such as the Academic Profile and CBASE were required so that data could be compared across the state.

Several institutions used the National Survey of Student Engagement (NSSE). These institutions indicated that they used the survey to assess students' perceptions regarding their level of engagement with faculty, their beliefs, and their values. The graduating-student survey,

99

student-satisfaction survey, and alumni survey were also widely used to gain a perspective on students' perceptions. A significant number of responses included other indirect approaches to measurement of core learning outcomes, such as case studies, focus groups, and syllabus analysis.

Essays, embedded questions, locally developed tests, standardized tests, and capstone courses were direct-measurement approaches that were popular among the 23 institutions that were assessing students' learning. Again, the criteria for these assignments as well as the rubrics used to grade them were key concerns.

The Extent to Which Assessment Led to Improvement

Fifty-nine percent of the respondents indicated that their assessment efforts led to changes. These changes ranged from curriculum changes to enhanced faculty involvement.

The areas of assessment-related changes most cited were 1) changes in curricula, 2) enhanced awareness of the value of assessment, 3) reevaluation of the assessment process, 4) enhanced faculty involvement, and 5) increased assessment training opportunities. The curriculum changes typically entailed adding a course or changing the sequence of a course. The enhancement of the value of assessment motivated administrators and faculty to reevaluate the current process and as a consequence seek the support of additional faculty members. The realization of the importance of assessment started a domino effect.

The acknowledgment of a need to foster faculty leadership in the assessment process is substantiated by the literature (Chapter 2: Faculty Engagement in Effective Assessment Strategies). The literature strongly communicated the critical nature of faculty members' engagement in the general education process, especially because the core curriculum does not belong to any single department.

The remaining respondents (41%) indicated that they had not implemented any changes based on assessment findings. These institutions variously noted that 1) assessment was course based and difficult to track; 2) 70% of enrollees were transfer students and had already completed the general education requirements elsewhere, and the data that were collected provided an overview; 3) data that were collected from a standardized examination did not provide enough evidence for change; 4) assessment was in the early stages and enough time had not elapsed to determine the effectiveness of the process; 5) a formal assessment process was in the development and initial implementation stages and that formal assessment would begin soon; and 6) no assessment process was in place.

The survey asked the respondents to discuss some of the positive activities that were ongoing in the institution. The results of the survey indicated that in some of the 23 institutions, positive activities relative to assessment of the general education curriculum were occurring. The overwhelming response was that the assessment process was being strengthened as faculty members recognized that learning outcomes needed to be clearer, baseline measures were available to be used as the basis for future assessment, and assessment training was increasingly available. Teaching was strengthened through the use of the active learning process, new centers for writing and mathematics, and the advocacy for the scholarship of assessment. Finally, the culture was being strengthened as the value of assessment was being embedded in the classroom, in the departments, in the colleges and schools, and in the institution.

This study provided information about how metropolitan and urban universities were doing in the area of identifying appropriate methodologies for formally assessing general education and to what extent they were using these data to implement changes. The results of the study strongly suggested that institutions that were seriously involved in the assessment process were realizing data-driven changes. The changes that were being made as a result of assessment ranged from adding new instructional materials to revising the curriculum. Universities whose faculty members collaborated and continued to look for better ways to assess student learning were experiencing a level of success.

It was critical that institutions properly aligned 1) the purpose of general education, 2) intended student-learning outcomes, 3) measurement approaches, and 4) assessment resources (faculty, training, funding, etc.) to optimize the assessment process. Finally, once data were collected and weaknesses identified in the pedagogy, curriculum, or the assessment process itself, changes should be implemented as soon as feasible. In doing so, institutions were assured that students would have the greatest opportunity to achieve academically and personally so that they might be able to contribute to society.

Stages of Assessment Implementation

Institutions were in five stages of conducting assessment. The schools were 1) actively engaged in the assessment process and making changes guided by assessment findings, 2) in the process of conducting assessment but unable to make changes based on collected data, 3) in the early stages of assessment but not yet able to make changes based on the collected data, 4) in the planning stages of the assessment process, or 5) not assessing the core curriculum, but had intentions to start doing so in the near future.

The institutions that were in stage one (assessing learning outcomes and making changes) of assessment implementation were able to make changes based on the findings of assessment.

102

The literature supports that this should be the case (American Association for Higher Education, 2004). Those who were in stage two knew that they needed to diversify their assessment methodologies. Stage three institutions (early stages) were confident that weaknesses would be identified; however, some of them knew that they needed additional methods to use for assessing the outcomes. It is important for the institutions in stages four and five to make progress towards implementing an assessment process (see Chapter 2: Assessment that Leads to Improvement).

Implications for Implementation of Assessment Process

The results of this study indicated that the assessment process for general education programs should include the following practices:

1. Faculty members should be an integral part of the planning for the assessment process. This involvement ensures that important input is received from key faculty members and that faculty members who teach courses that are part of the core curriculum are fully engaged in developing the process. (See Chapter 2: Faculty Engagement in Effective Assessment Strategies.)

2. Clear purposes should be established for the assessment process. Once the purpose is determined, the learning outcomes can be clearly articulated. (See Chapter 2: Principles of an Effective General Education Program.)

3. Measurement approaches should be directly linked to the learning outcome being assessed. For example, if writing is being assessed, students should be given an opportunity to demonstrate their writing skills in an appropriate way. (See Chapter 2: Methods of Assessment: Identification of Effective Measurement Approaches.)

4. When choosing measurement approaches, a mixture of direct and indirect approaches should be sought. This mixture leads to the acquisition of richer data. (See Chapter 2: Methods of Assessment: Identification of Effective Measurement Approaches.)

5. Criteria for assignments that will be graded for assessment purposes should be shared among all faculty members who are involved with the particular learning outcome. This collaboration creates a heightened awareness regarding what is to be taught (both content and teaching strategies).

6. Criteria for assignments should be shared with all of the students on a regular basis. This inclusion creates a heightened awareness regarding intended student-learning outcomes.

7. Faculty members should carefully consider rubrics and reevaluate them on a regular basis. This review ensures uniformity in grading.

8. Because general education programs do not belong to any one department, the interdisciplinary approach should be fostered in the assessment process. (See Chapter 2: Principles of an Effective General Education Program.)

9. Results of assessment should be shared with key stakeholders so that they will know how students are doing in their academic achievements and personal growth. Sharing results also informs stakeholders regarding teaching effectiveness. (See Chapter 2: Principles of an Effective General Education Program.)

10. Tracking measurement approaches that yield data that lead to improvement should be an ongoing activity so that future assessment can be informed.

11. Institutions should reevaluate, on a regular basis, the assessment process for general education programs' continuous improvement. (See Chapter 2: Principles of an Effective General Education Program.)

12. The positive activities that are ongoing as a result of assessment should be acknowledged. This recognition will lead to a heightened awareness of the value of assessment.

13. Institutions should strongly consider the significance of faculty involvement for the successful implementation of assessment and act accordingly (release time, training, recognition of efforts, etc.)

It is important that institutions realize what stage they are in the implementation phase of the assessment process for the following reasons:

1. Funding opportunities for enhancement of the assessment process and implementation of plans to address weaknesses in the pedagogy, curriculum, and assessment practices (Banta et al., 1996; Callahan et al., 2001; Ewell, 2001)

2. Greater awareness on the part of institutions' leadership of what is needed to enhance institutions' continuous quality improvement initiatives if they have a clear understanding of what stage the school is in at a given time

3. Funding appropriations for training

4. Seeking mentoring opportunities

5. Accreditation of the institution (Commission on Colleges—Southern Accreditation of Colleges and Schools [SACS] Website, n.d.)

6. Students' perceptions of the institution (students most likely will have greater respect for institutions that are in stage one of the assessment process).

7. Employers' perception of the institution (employers most likely will have greater respect for institutions that are in stage one of the assessment process) (Miller, 1990; Palomba & Banta, 1999)

8. Parents' perception of the institution (parents most likely will have greater respect for institutions that are in stage one of the assessment process).

Recommendations for Future Research

This study was conducted in order to learn more about the assessment process used in higher education at 54 institutions that were all members of the Coalition of Urban and Metropolitan Universities. The foci of the study were to determine a) the measurement approaches used to assess core curricula and b) to what extent these approaches to measurement are producing data that can be used to make changes for improvement purposes.

The results of the study indicated that 16 institutions or 59% of the 27 respondents were able to use their assessment results to make changes. The remaining 41% of the respondents were unable to report that they had made changes. The predominant reasons that were cited for not being able to make changes were that there was no formal assessment process or that the assessment process was just beginning and enough time had not passed for meaningful evaluation.

Following is a list of recommendations for future research.

1. Conduct a study using the institutions in this study that did not report any changes but were in the early stages and planning stages of assessment. The focus of the study would be to determine the effectiveness of the newly implemented assessment measures. [See Chapter 3: Research Design (theoretical sampling)]

2. Conduct a follow-up study to determine how the original 16 institutions that reported changes were progressing in their assessment efforts. (Theoretical Sampling)

3. Conduct a study on specific measurement approaches to find out the type of changes that were made as a result of using these measurements to assess student-learning outcomes.

4. Conduct a comparative study to determine if there is a difference in the way student-learning outcomes are measured at metropolitan and urban universities and other types of institutions.

5. Conduct a comparative study to determine if there is a difference in purpose and core learning outcome between metropolitan and urban universities and other types of institutions.

6. Conduct a study to determine if interdisciplinary approaches to assessment of general education programs make a major impact on changes.

7. Conduct a study to examine the effectiveness of longitudinal assessment. The focus of this study would be to determine the effectiveness of the core curriculum in student development (readiness for the workplace and personal growth) over a period of time (3–4 years).

8. Conduct a follow-up study to determine which measures resulted, over time, in the most significant increases in student-learning outcomes.

9. Conduct a study to determine the differences that exist among institutions in the assessment methodologies used to assess student-learning outcomes based on the associated accrediting body.

APPENDIX A

LIST OF INSTITUTIONS

Institutions and Enrollment

Institution	Enrollment
Boise State University	18,700
California State University - Fresno	21,389
California State University - Hayward	13,240
California State University - Sacramento	28,375
California State University - San Bernardino	16,000
Cleveland State University	16,000
Eastern Michigan University	23,710
Florida International University	34,000
Indiana University Northwest	5,097
Indiana University Purdue University Indianapolis	28,496
Kennesaw State University	17,485
Louisiana State University in Shreveport	4,230
Metropolitan State College of Denver	20,230
Metropolitan State University	6,010
Northern Kentucky University	11,500
Pace University	13,498
Portland State University	21,275
Rutgers-Newark, The State University of New Jersey	10,346
San Jose State University	30,000
Southern Illinois University - Edwardsville	10,014
Southwest Missouri State University	19,000
Southwest Texas State University	26,366
Towson University	16,000
University of Alaska at Anchorage	20,337
University of Arkansas at Little Rock	11,000
University of Central Florida	41,102
University of Colorado at Denver	
University of Colorado, Colorado Springs	11,000
University of Connecticut - Tri-Campus	25,842
University of Houston - Downtown	10,528
University of Houston System	10,404
University of Illinois at Chicago	25,228
University of Massachusetts at Boston	12,394
University of Memphis	18,883
University of Missouri - Kansas City	14,244

Institution	Enrollment
University of Missouri - St. Louis	
University of Nebraska at Omaha	14,100
University of Nevada - Las Vegas	24,000
University of North Carolina at Charlotte	18,000
University of North Carolina at Greensboro	14,000
University of North Florida	14,000
University of North Texas System	29,714
University of Rhode Island	13,435
University of South Carolina - Spartanburg	4,396
University of South Florida	41,392
University of South Florida - St. Petersburg	4,000
University of Southern Indiana	9,899
University of Southern Maine	11,382
University of Tennessee at Chattanooga	7,137
University of Texas at San Antonio	24,000
University of Toledo	20,594
University of Washington, Tacoma	2,000
University of Wisconsin, Milwaukee	25,000
Virginia Commonwealth University	25,001
Washburn University of Topeka	6,000
Washington State University- Spokane	752
Washington State University- Vancouver	1,910
Widener University	2,180
William Paterson University	11,200
Wright State University	16,000
Youngstown State University	12,000

APPENDIX B

COVER LETTER

Angela R. Albert
Doctoral Candidate
University of Central Florida
402 S. Winsome Ct.
Lake Mary, FL 32746
407-882-0281 (daytime) or 407-328-9380 (evening)
aalbert@mail.ucf.edu

Dear General Education Assessment Coordinator:

This survey is being administered in an effort to learn more about your experiences in assessing general education at your institution. At the conclusion of this study, additional knowledge about assessment efforts that are currently taking place at the 62 institutions that are members of The Coalition of Urban and Metropolitan Colleges and Universities will be available for those seeking to enhance their assessment processes in the area of general education. I will provide you with a copy of the results from this study. Your participation is greatly needed.

I am asking that you respond to the six open-ended questions in the attached questionnaire by describing, in your own words, aspects of the current general education assessment process at your respective institution.

There are two options for responding to the questionnaire. You may choose to use the hardcopy version of the questionnaire, or you may choose to use the web-based version located at http://oeas.ucf.edu/angela_doc.htm. If you choose to use the web-based version, it is advisable to first create your responses in a Word document and then cut and paste your text into the text boxes on the web. You cannot go back to your document on the web once you have submitted it.

However, if you choose to respond by using the hardcopy questionnaire, upon completion, please send the questionnaire with your typed or written responses in the self-addressed stamped envelope. It will take approximately 45 minutes to complete the questionnaire. I am asking that, if at all possible, that you return the questionnaire by November 30, 2003.

Please be assured that all of the data will be presented in a way that preserves your institution's anonymity. Also, feel free to contact me at the above phone number if you have any questions or concerns as you go through the questionnaire.

Again, your participation is very important to this study, as the results of this research will add significantly to the existing scholarship of assessment. I look forward to your involvement!

Respectfully,
Angela R. Albert
Doctoral Candidate
University of Central Florida

APPENDIX C

FIRST ELECTRONIC MAIL MESSAGE

Hello: Thanks for agreeing to participate in my study. I have included parts of the letter that I sent to you via U. S. mail and hope that you will decide to respond by using the web-based survey. If you have had problems accessing the web-survey, please try again, as I have taken care of the glitch that was there.

This survey is being administered in an effort to learn more about your experiences in assessing general education at your institution. At the conclusion of this study, additional knowledge about assessment efforts that are currently taking place at the 62 institutions that are members of The Coalition of Urban and Metropolitan Colleges and Universities will be available for those seeking to enhance their assessment processes in the area of general education. I will provide you with a copy of the results from this study. Your participation is greatly needed.

I am asking that you respond to the six open-ended questions by describing, in your own words, aspects of the current general education assessment process at your respective institution.

There are two options for responding to the questionnaire. You may choose to use the hardcopy version of the questionnaire, or you may choose to use the web-based version located at http://oeas.ucf.edu/angela_doc.htm. If you choose to use the web-based version, it is advisable to first create your responses in a Word document and then cut and paste your text into the text boxes on the web. You cannot go back to your document on the web once you have submitted it.

Please be assured that all of the data will be presented in a way that preserves your institution's anonymity. Also, feel free to contact me at the above phone number if you have any questions or concerns as you go through the questionnaire.

Again, your participation is very important to this study, as the results of this research will add significantly to the existing scholarship of assessment. I look forward to your involvement!

"From Promise to Prominence: Celebrating 40 Years of Service to Students"

Angela R. Albert
Assistant Director
University of Central Florida
Operational Excellence &
Assessment Support
12424 Research Parkway,
Ste. 225
Orlando, FL 32826-3207
aalbert@mail.ucf.edu
Phone: (407) 882-0281
Fax: (407) 882-0288

APPENDIX D

SECOND ELECTRONIC MAIL MESSAGE

Dear Colleagues:

I appreciate those of you who have already responded to my questionnaire. As you already know, this study is one that will provide information about how institutions, within the Coalition of Urban and Metropolitan Universities, are assessing their general education programs and the improvements that are being implemented as a consequence.

If you have not already responded, I look forward to you using the web-based survey at http://oeas.ucf.edu/angela_doc.htm. Just remember that you cannot go back and add to the survey once you have started, so you might want to copy and paste the survey in Word and then cut and paste your responses when you have completely addressed each question. You may also respond by using the hardcopy version and returning it in the self-addressed envelope that I have provided. If you have any questions or concerns about the study or your role in the stud, please do not hesitate to contact me at 407-882-0281 or email me at aalbert@mail.ucf.edu.

I look forward to hearing from those of you who have not yet found the time or the opportunity to complete the questionnaire.

Again, thanks to those of you who have already provided information and data!

Respectfully,

Angela R. Albert
Assistant Director
University of Central Florida
Operational Excellence &
Assessment Support
12424 Research Parkway,
Ste. 225
Orlando, FL 32826-3207
aalbert@mail.ucf.edu
Phone: (407) 882-0281
Fax: (407) 882-0288

APPENDIX E

THIRD ELECTRONIC MAIL MESSAGE

January 13, 2004

Today I am taking a risk of seeming like a pest to once again request that you take some time

out of your busy schedule to assist me in my research efforts.

To recap my research, the focus of my research is to learn more about your experiences in assessing general education at your institution. At the conclusion of this study, additional knowledge about assessment efforts that are currently taking place at the 62 institutions that are members of The Coalition of Urban and Metropolitan Colleges and Universities will be available for those seeking to enhance their assessment processes in the area of general education. I will provide you with a copy of the results from this study.

I am asking that you respond to the six open-ended questions by describing, in your own words, aspects of the current general education assessment process at your respective institution. Even if you are unable to answer all of my questions, it would be very helpful if you would provide answers that describe your current situation regarding general education program assessment.

If you choose to use the web-based version, it is advisable to first create your responses in a Word document and then cut and paste your text into the text boxes on the web. You cannot go back to your document on the web once you have submitted it.

If you are ready to start, click here: http://oeas.ucf.edu/angela_doc.htm.

Please be assured that all of the data will be presented in a way that preserves your institution's anonymity. Also, feel free to contact me at the number shown below if you have any questions or concerns as you go through the questionnaire.

Again, your participation is very important to this study, as the results of this research will add significantly to the existing scholarship of assessment. I look forward to your involvement!

UCF Doctoral Candidate

"From Promise to Prominence: Celebrating 40 Years of Service to Students"

Angela R. Albert
Assistant Director
University of Central Florida
Operational Excellence &
Assessment Support
12424 Research Parkway,
Ste. 225
Orlando, FL 32826-3207
aalbert@mail.ucf.edu
Phone: (407) 882-0281
Fax: (407) 882-0288

APPENDIX F

QUESTIONNAIRE

QUESTIONNAIRE

Your completing this questionnaire constitutes your informed consent. You are free to refuse to answer any questions and you may stop the questionnaire at any time.

Note: For the purposes of this study, assessment may be generally defined as the ongoing, systematic planning and development of goals and learning outcomes, the collection of data, the documentation of results, and the continual improvement of academic programs.

Name of Institution: _____

1. Briefly provide a description of the purpose of your general education program?

2. What core general education student-learning outcomes have been developed and are being measured at your institution? For example, the ability to think critically, the ability to communicate effectively both written and verbal, the ability to solve quantitative problems, etc.

3. What types of measurement approaches (instruments, data collection methods) are being used to assess these core student-learning outcomes at your institution? For example, portfolios, standardized tests, essays, embedded test questions, etc.

120

4. Which core student learning outcome measurement instruments and data collection methods have yielded the type of data that has made it possible to make improvements in your general education program, including curricula changes, specific course revisions, teaching strategies, etc.?

5. Describe improvements that have been made at your institutions as a result of data collected from core student learning outcomes assessment. For example, revised course content, revised curriculum, different delivery of instruction, etc.

6. As you assess your General Education Program and analyze the results, have you learned that there are some positive things that you are doing that are effective in the program? If yes, briefly describe those positive strategies.

If you have documentation of the general education goals and structural framework (basic foundations), please include it with this completed questionnaire. If you choose to use the web-based survey, please provide the website address of your general education program or forward the literature to me in the enclosed envelope.

Your institution's General Education website address: _____

In an effort to gain a more thorough understanding of the general education student learning outcome assessment process at your institution, I would like to follow-up with a telephone interview using this questionnaire as the basis for more in depth questions. If you would be willing to participate in a 15-20 minute phone interview, please provide me with contact information (Name, Phone and Email address) on a separate sheet.

Thank you for your participation in this study.
You may use the back of this questionnaire to add comments.

APPENDIX G

OPEN CODING LIST

Hermeneutic Unit: generaleducationassessment

*fac involv pos + interdisc
*meaningful measurements + positive ..
Academic Profile.
ACT Exam
activ lng strat pos
add cours
add crs
all of the assessments mean
alumni survey
amer insti.
anal ski
annual ass rep - mean
annul step for goal achvmnt pos
art
assess crit improv
assess res excellent no change mean
assessment retreat
baseline measures pos
behavior scie
br
CAAP
capstone
case stud
cbase
cert licen exam
challenge-breath
challenge-transfer studens
challenge-variability of courses
challenge crs based assess
change class sz improv
changed level of crs
changing the textbook
classroom assess
collab w/others
collab. lng
comm-wr-or
common academic experience
community service
comparable to other grads pos
comparing outcomes to curriculum
contemporary issues
coopt adher w/dissid pos
coopt diss w/impor role - pos

123

cours bsd
cours grds
creat task force/committee improv
crs bsd-mean
crs bsd assessment
CT
CTl anal ski l comm-or-wr l cul app l tech
cult awar
data not specific enough to make improvemens improv
dec mkg
degree audit
dep l br
diagnostic testing upon entering
dir observ
div
economic
emb ques
environ apprec
esl classes improv
ess
essay mean
ethics
ETS
fac involv pos
facul schol
focus grp
for lang
future plans
general pol,econ,soci,psych
general social
geography
glob awar
GPAs
Graduating Senior Survey
guidelines for gened courses improv
high stakes
history
humanities
impl fac workshops
improv execut
improv tech pos
incrsd awrness of core otcmes improv
indepen thnkr
independent thinkers
info literacy

integra stu and insti port
interdisc
interdisc pos
interrelat - sci,tech, socie
interrelat -phys,mental,emo and qual of lfe
intgrt gened gls in capstone pos
intrpt quan & qual data
leadership ski
learner centered
life lng lrn
listening
low stakes
math center
Measure of Intellectual Development
National Survey of Student Engagement
new appro to assess
new gened prgrm
new writing and math center pos
No response
no sig curr changes
nyk
peer revw
perform
pers grow
political
port
port institu
port mean
port meaningful
pre/post
prob sol
prob sol l pers gr
promote and enhance lrng
pscyhological
quant
ramifications for noncompliance
reading
realize assessment works pos
realize otcm not well dfnd pos
reasoning
reevaltn of crs
reexam gened improv
rep prog public pos]
res tools
research paper

resesearch tools
resolution-registerandassess around the same time pos
results for curricula and pedagogy improv
reten rate
retention rates
rev course
rev curr
rev gened
rev lrng outco
rev pedagogy
schol of teach
science
self lrn
senior assign mean
significant # of transfer students
soci awar
social science
specialized reading course improv
stan test
stand test
stud sat svy
stud/activ log
suc cmplt of crs
succ in societ
surv
surv mean
surve fac
survey-loc
survey-nat
syl anal
synthes info
technology
test-state
test loc
tests
tools for know
val ethi
workshops implemen
world civil.

Hermeneutic Unit – General Education2

agreement on faculty
align courses with objectives
conducting meaningful assessment

126

faculty involvement
focus on improvement
future plans
interdisciplinary
optimistic attitude
planning by faculty
realizes challenges
scholarship of assessment
seek faculty input
variety of approaches

Hermeneutic Unit: gened4

improv
lng comm
meaningful meas
not yet known

APPENDIX H

IRB APPROVAL FORMS

University of
Central Florida

August 13, 2003

Angela R. Albert
University of Central Florida
Operational Excellence & Assessment Support
12424 Research Parkway, Ste. 225
Orlando, FL 32826-3207

Dear Ms. Albert:

With reference to your protocol entitled, "A Qualitative Study of Assessment Methods Used to Measure Student Learning Outcomes in General Education at Urban and Metropolitan Universities," I am enclosing for your records the approved, executed document of the UCFIRB Form you had submitted to our office.

Please be advised that this approval is given for one year. Should there be any addendums or administrative changes to the already approved protocol, they must also be submitted to the Board. Changes should not be initiated until written IRB approval is received. Adverse events should be reported to the IRB as they occur. Further, should there be a need to extend this protocol, a renewal form must be submitted for approval at least one month prior to the anniversary date of the most recent approval and is the responsibility of the investigator (UCF).

Should you have any questions, please do not hesitate to call me at 823-2901.

Please accept our best wishes for the success of your endeavors.

Cordially,

Chris Grayson
Institutional Review Board (IRB)

Copies: Dr. Mary Ann Lynn
        IRB File

Office of Research
12443 Research Parkway Suite 207 • Orlando, FL 32826-3252
407-823-3778 • FAX 407-823-3299
An Equal Opportunity and Affirmative Action Institution

IRB COMMITTEE APPROVAL FORM
FOR UCF/OOR/IRB USE ONLY

PI(s) Name: Angela Albert
Title: A Qualitative Study of Assessment Methods Used to Measure Student Learning Outcomes in General Education at Urban and Metropolitan Universities.

Check as applicable (optional):

[ ]Yes [ ]No
Have sufficient assurances been given to the committee to establish that the potential value of this research exceeds the risks involved?

[ ]Yes [ ]No
Written and oral presentations must be given to participating subjects (parents or guardians, if minors) informing them of the protocol, possible risks involved, the value of the research, and the right to withdraw at any time.

[ ]Yes [ ]No
A signed written consent must be obtained for each human subject participant.

[ ]Yes [ ]No
Are cooperating institutions involved? If yes, was there a sheet attached providing the name of the institutions, the number and status of participants, name of the involved official of the institution, telephone, and other pertinent information?

Committee Members:

Dr. Theodore Angelopoulos: _____
Ms. Sandra Browdy: _____
Dr. Jacqui Byers: _____

[ ] Contingent Approval
Dated: _____

Dr. Ratna Chakrabarti: _____
Dr. Karen Dennis: _____
Dr. Barbara Fritzsche: _____

[ ] Final Approval
Dated: _____

Dr. Robert Kennedy: _____
Dr. Gene Lee: _____
Ms. Gail McKinney: _____
Dr. Debra Reinhart: _____
Dr. Valerie Sims: _____
Dr. Bob Spina: _____

[X] Expedited
Dated: 7 August 2003

Chair, IRB

Signed: _____
Dr. Sophia Dziegielewski

[ ] Exempt
Dated: _____

LIST OF REFERENCES

Abrahamson, C. E., & Kimsey, W. D. (2002). General education, interdisciplinary pedagogy and the process of content transformation. *Education, 122*(3), 587–588.

American Association for Higher Education. (2004). Mission statement. Retrieved January 10, 2004, from http://www.aahe.org/newdirections/vision.htm

Angelo, T. A. (2002). Engaging and supporting faculty in the scholarship of assessment: Guidelines from research and best practice. In T. W. Banta (Ed.), *Building a scholarship of assessment* (pp. 185–200). San Francisco: Jossey-Bass.

Association of American Colleges and Universities. (1994). *Strong foundations: Twelve principles for effective general education programs.* Washington, DC: Association of American Colleges and Universities.

Association of American Colleges and Universities Website (n.d.). Retrieved June 23, 2003, from http://www.aacu-edu.org/

Banta, T. W. (1993). Is there hope for TQM in the academy? In D. L. Hubbard (Ed.), *Continuous quality improvement: Making the transition to education* (pp. 143–157). Maryville, MO: Prescott.

Banta, T. W., Lund, J.P., Black, K. E., & Oblander, F. W. (1996). *Assessment in practice: Putting principles to work on college campuses.* San Francisco: Jossey-Bass.

Bauer, K. W., & Frawley, W. J. (2002). *General education curriculum revisions and assessment at a research university.* Paper presented at the 2002 Association of Institutional Research (AIR) Conference, Toronto, Canada.

Benjamin, R., & Chun, M. (2003). A new field of dreams: The collegiate learning assessment project. *Peer Review, 5*(4) . Retrieved December 3, 2003, from http://www.aacu.org/peerreview/pr-su03/pr-su03feature2.cfm

Borman, K. M., LeCompte, M. D., & Goetz, J. P. (1986). Ethnographic and qualitative research design and why it doesn't work. *American Behavioral Scientist, 30*(1), 42–57.

Brown, S., & Glasner, A. (1999). *Assessment matters in higher education: Choosing and using diverse approaches.* Philadelphia: SRHE and Open University Press
Callahan, P. M., Doyle, W., & Finney, J. E. (2001). Evaluating state higher education performance: Measuring up 2000. *Change 33*(2), 10–19.

Center for Education. (2001). *Knowing what students know: The science and design of educational assessment.* Washington, DC: National Academies Press. Retrieved December 19, 2003 from http://lab.nap.edu/books/0309072727/html/index.html

131

Charmaz, K. (2000). Grounded theory: Objectivist and constructivist methods. In N. Denzin & Y. S. Lincoln (Eds.), *Handbook of qualitative research* (2nd ed., pp. 509–535). Thousand Oaks, CA: Sage.

Chun, M. (2002, Winter/Spring). Looking where the light is better: A review of the literature on assessing higher education quality. *Peer Review 4*(2/3), 16–25.

Coalition of Urban & Metropolitan Universities Website. (n.d.). Retrieved October 13, 2003, from http://cumu.uc.iupui.edu/directory.asp

Commission on Colleges—Southern Association of Colleges and Schools. (2004). Principles of accreditation: Foundations for quality enhancement. Retrieved February 23, 2004, from http://www.sacscoc.org/pdf/principles%20of%20accreditation1.pdf

Cooperative Institutional Research Program (CIRP). (n.d.). Retrieved April 7, 2003, from http://www.gseis.ucla.edu/heri/cirp.html

Cornesky, R. (1993). *The quality professor*. Madison, WI: Magna.

Cornesky, R., McCool, S., Byrnes, L., & Weber, R. (1992). *Institutional quality index: Implementing total quality management in higher education*. Madison, WI: Magna.

Creswell, J. W. (1998). *Qualitative inquiry and research design: Choosing among five traditions*. Thousand Oaks, CA: Sage.

Dilman, D. A. (2000). *Mail and Internet surveys: The tailored design method*. New York: Wiley.

Dressel, P. L., & Mayhew, L. B. (1954). *General education: Explorations in evaluation*. Washington, DC: American Council on Education.

Evenbeck, S., & Kahn, S. (2001). Enhancing learning assessment and accountability through communities of practice. *Change, 33*(3), 24–34.

Ewell, P. T. (1995). Assessment of higher education quality: Promise and politics. In S. J. Messick (Educational Testing Service) (Ed.), *Assessment in higher education: Issues of access, quality, student development and public policy* (pp. 147–156). Mahwah, NJ: Lawrence Erlbaum.

Ewell, P. T. (2001). Statewide testing in higher education. *Change, 33*(2), 21–23.

Ewell, P. T. (2002). An emerging scholarship: A brief history of assessment. In T. W. Banta (Ed.), *Building a scholarship of assessment* (pp. 3–26). San Francisco: Jossey-Bass.

Ferren, A. S. (2003). The dollars and sense behind general education reform. *Peer Review 5*(4). Retrieved December 3, 2003, from http://www.aacu.org/peerreview/pr-su03/pr-su03feature1.cfm

Gaff, J. G. (1993). Toward a second wave of reform. In N. A. Raisman (Ed.), *Directing general education outcomes* (pp. 5–12). San Francisco: Jossey- Bass.

Gaff, J. G. (1999). *General education: The changing agenda.* Washington, DC: Association of American Colleges and Universities.

Gaff, J. G. (2003, Summer). Keeping general education vital: A struggle against original sin? *Peer Review, 5*(4). Retrieved December 3, 2003, from http://www.aacu.org/peerreview/pr-su03/pr-su03reality.cfm

Grob, L., & Kuehl, J. R. (1997). Coherence and assessment in a general education program. *Liberal Education 83*(1). Retrieved February 26, 2003, from http://web4.epnet.com/citation.asp?tb=1&_ug=dbs+0+In+en%2Dus...

Huba, M. E., & Freed, J. E. (2000). *Learner-centered assessment on college campuses: Shifting the focus from teaching to learning.* Needham Heights, MA: Pearson.

Hubbard, D. L. (1993). Is quality a manageable commodity in higher education? In D. L. Hubbard (Ed.), *Continuous quality improvement: Making the transition to education* (pp. 72–89). Maryville, MO: Prescott.

Humphreys, D. (1997). *General education and American commitments: A national report on diversity courses and requirements.* Washington, DC: Association of American Colleges and Universities.

Kanter, S. L., Gamson, Z. F., & London, H. B. (1997). *Revitalizing general education in a time of scarcity: A navigational chart for administrators and faculty.* Needham Heights, MA: Allyn & Bacon.

Kiger, D. M. (1996). Self-assessing general education outcomes at a community college. *Community College Review, 23*(4), ii. Retrieved February 26, 2003, from http://web4.epnet.com/citation.asp?tb=1&_ug=dbs+0+1n+en%2Dus

Kuh, G. D. (2001). Assessing what really matters to student learning: Inside the national survey of student engagement. *Change, 33*(3), 10–17.

Kuh, G. D. (2003). What we're learning about engagement from NSSE: Benchmarks for effective educational practices. *Change, 35*(2), 24–32.

Lane, C. (n.d). Blooms taxonomy. In *The distance learning technology resource guide*. The Education Coalition. Retrieved January 11, 2004, from http://www.tecweb.org/eddevel/edtech/blooms.html

Lewis, R. G., & Smith, D. H. (1994). *Total quality in higher education*. Delray Beach, FL: St. Lucie Press.

Maki, P. (2001). From standardized tests to alternative methods: Some current resources on methods to assess learning in general education. *Change, 33*(2), 29–31.

Maki, P. (2002). Moving from paperwork to pedagogy: Channeling intellectual curiosity into a commitment to assessment. *AAHE Bulletin, May 2002*. Retrieved November 10, 2003, from http://www.aahebulletin.com/public/archive/paperwork.asp

Maki, P. (2003). Dialogue fuels assessment. *AAHE Inquiry & Action, Summer 2003*, 1–6.

Mayhew, L. B., Ford, P. J., & Hubbard, D. L. (1990). *The quest for quality*. San Francisco: Jossey-Bass.

Miles, M. B., & Huberman, A. M. (1994). *Qualitative data analysis*. Thousand Oaks, CA: Sage.

Miller, R. (1990). *Major American higher education issues and challenges in the 1990s*. London: Jessica Kingsley.

Morse, J. M., & Richards, L. (2002). *Readme first for a user's guide to qualitative methods*. Thousand Oaks, CA: Sage.

Muffo, J. (2001). Institutional effectiveness, student learning and outcomes assessment. In R. D. Howards (Ed.), *Institutional research: Decision support in higher education* (pp. 60–87). Tallahassee, FL: Association for Institutional Research.

National Center for Education Statistics. (2000). *The NPEC sourcebook on assessment, Volume 1: Definitions and assessment methods for critical thinking, problem solving, and writing*. (NCES 2000–172). Washington, DC: U. S. Government Printing Office.

National Center for Education Statistics. (2002). *Digest of education statistics, 2002*. Retrieved August 14, 2003, from http://nces.ed.gov/pubsearch/pubsinfo.asp?pubid=2003060

National Center for Postsecondary Improvement. (2001). Report to stakeholders on the condition and effectiveness of postsecondary education. *Change 33*(3), 24–26.

North Central Association of Colleges and Schools—Higher Learning Commission Website. (n.d.). Retrieved January 11, 2004, from http://www.ncahigherlearningcommission.org/commission/index.htm

Palomba, C. A. (2001). Implementing effective assessment. In C.A. Palomba & T. W. Banta (Eds.), *Assessing student competence in accredited disciplines* (pp. 13–28). Sterling, VA: Stylus.

Palomba, C. A. (2002). Scholarly assessment of student learning in the major and general education. In T. W. Banta (Ed.), *Building a scholarship of assessment* (pp. 201–222). San Francisco: Jossey-Bass.

Palomba, C. A., & Banta, T. W. (1999). *Assessment essentials: Planning, implementing, and improving assessment in higher education.* San Francisco: Jossey-Bass.

Patten, M. (2000). *Understanding research methods.* Los Angeles: Pyrczak.

Pike, G. R. (2002). Methods of assessment: Measurement issues in outcomes assessment. In T. W. Banta (Ed.), *Building a scholarship of assessment* (pp. 131–147). San Francisco: Jossey-Bass.

Posovac, E. J., & Carey, R. G. (1997). *Program evaluation methods and case studies.* Upper Saddle River, NJ: Prentice Hall.

Ratcliff, J. L., Johnson, D. K., La Nasa, S. M., & Gaff, J. G. (2000). *The status of general education in the year 2000: Summary of a national survey.* Washington, DC: Association of American Colleges and Universities.

Romero, M. (2001). Define the role of state systems. The academy in transition: General education in an age of student mobility. Fifth series of discussion papers for faculty members and academic leaders. Washington, DC: Association of American Colleges and Universities.

Schoenberg, R. (2001). Why do I have to take this course? Credit hours, transfer and curricular coherence. The academy in transition: General education in an age of student mobility. Fifth series of discussion papers for faculty members and academic leaders. Washington, DC: Association of American Colleges and Universities.

Seymour, D. T. (1993). *On Q: Causing quality in higher education.* Phoenix, AZ: Oryx Press.

Siegel, M. J. (2003). *Primer on assessment of the first year of college.* Brevard, NC: Policy Center on the First Year of College.

Stone, J., & Friedman, S. (2002). A case study in the integration of assessment and general education: Lessons learned from a complex process. *Assessment & Evaluation in Higher Education, 27*(2), 199–210.

Strauss, A., & Corbin, J. (1990). *Basics of qualitative research: Grounded theory procedures and techniques.* Newbury Park, CA: Sage.

135

Strauss, A., & Corbin, J. (1997). *Grounded theory in practice*. Thousand Oaks, CA: Sage.

Strauss, A., & Corbin, J. (1998). *Basics of qualitative research: Techniques and procedures for developing grounded theory*. Thousand Oaks, CA: Sage.

Walvoord, B. E., & Anderson, V. J. (1998). *Effective grading: A tool for learning and assessment*. San Francisco: Jossey-Bass.

Weinstein, C. E., & Van Mater Stone, G. (1993). Broadening our conception of general education: The self-regulated learner. In N. A. Raisman (Ed.), *Directing general education outcomes* (pp. 31–39). San Francisco: Jossey-Bass.